Taking Up Cruising

John Davies is an experienced cruising yachtsman. This is a practical, comprehensive guide for
all those taking up cruising, with full instructions
on cost, maintenance and techniques.

JOHN DAVIES

Taking Up Cruising

DRAWINGS BY
Fid Harnack S.M.A.

STANLEY PAUL
London

STANLEY PAUL & CO LTD
178–202 Great Portland Street, London W1

AN IMPRINT OF THE  HUTCHINSON GROUP

London Melbourne Sydney
Auckland Bombay Toronto
Johannesburg New York

★

First published 1966

*This book has been set in Baskerville, printed in Great Britain
on Antique Wove paper by Anchor Press, and
bound by Wm. Brendon, both of Tiptree, Essex*

Contents

Illustrations

I

What Sort of Yacht Do You Want?

WHEN I wrote in a recent book that in my opinion 'dinghy sailing is simply a complicated way of getting wet', I expected a roar of outrage from my son, who has been sailing half out of a National Twelve for a good many years now. Instead he merely said, and then only as though he felt it was required of him, 'Of course, you don't know what you're talking about.' And he even added, 'I suppose there may be something in this cruising lark after all.'

Thinking about that, I realised that a lot of sailing men probably undergo a sea change at about my son's age (he is twenty-six). Until somewhere around then they are dinghy fanatics. Some, of course, remain so for much longer, a minority all their lives. But for most there comes a time when the excitements of bashing round the buoys are exchanged for the different delights of cruising.

Both kinds of sailing have the same basic ingredient, namely a love of exercising one of the most basic and satisfying of all skills, that of bending the elements to one's will. Dinghy sailing is largely concerned, apart from this, with competing against one's fellows, whereas in cruising the competition is more wholly a matter of battling against the elements themselves, for longer periods and often in far tougher

conditions. There is also the added thrill of exploration and
the satisfaction of being self-sufficient and self-dependent—
with no rescue launch on hand. Moreover, cruising appeals
to the older and more mature man's desire to escape, if only
for a while, from the problems and complexities of land-
bound life; for solitude, simplicity, and peace.

Everyone interested in sailing knows that since the last
war there has been a phenomenal increase in the number of
men (and women) who go down to the sea in small boats.
The great sailing explosion immediately after the war was
mainly in the dinghy classes, for the simple reason that
dinghies are comparatively cheap, easily transportable, and
can be sailed on pretty well any bit of water that happens
to be handy. But this got a lot of people afloat, and it was a
natural development that, after some years of tearing around
more or less within sight of the clubhouse, many of these
dinghy sailors should start to feel the urge to venture further
in something bigger. The result has been a secondary explosion in the cruising world. There is plenty of proof of this
in the proliferation of ads for small cruising craft which one
finds in the sailing journals nowadays.

It seemed to me, therefore, that there was a good case for
a book on cruising for this sort of person, i.e. for the man
who already knows the fundamentals of how to handle a
boat under sail, but who is now coming to cruising for the
first time. It should therefore be a fairly elementary sort of
book, from the cruising point of view. It should not try to
cover every aspect, including celestial navigation in two
pages. Only a small percentage of cruising men, even among
those who have been many years at the game, have ever used
a sextant, or even held one in their hands. Only a minority
have ever 'been foreign'; indeed, a lot have never been out
of sight of land, except inadvertently, when it rained hard
or a sea mist came in. The great majority are quite content
just to pootle from one landmark or seamark to another up
and down their particular bit of coast.

It is primarily for the latter that this book is intended.

And if it adds anything to their enjoyment of the sport they are now taking up, and helps them to get there and back on their week-end trips or their summer holiday cruises safely and reasonably efficiently, it will have achieved its purpose.

But enough of this preliminary chatter. Let's get under way.

First of all, and fairly obviously, before you can go cruising you must have a boat to go in :

CHOOSING A CRUISING BOAT

The first question to be answered here is : what sort of boat will suit you best? And the answer to this depends upon the answers to three other questions which are to some extent interrelated. These are :

1. Where will you sail, and what sort of sailing will you be doing?

2. How big a boat should you start off with?

3. Should you aim to buy a new boat or a second-hand one?

(1) *Where will you sail?*

This question is of much greater importance to the cruising man than it is to the dinghy sailor. As we have seen already, it is possible to sail a dinghy on almost any stretch of water that is both conveniently and legally accessible. The cruising man's choice is much more limited. In fact, he may not have a choice at all. For one thing, he's got to go to the coast, unless he's lucky enough to live there already—the dinghy man's many inland sailing grounds are out as far as he is concerned. For another, he's got to have a base—i.e. a mooring or a berth where he can leave his boat, unless she is small enough to trail to and from home, and even then it will be a considerable labour to do this every time he wants to sail. It is also desirable that the area in which he sails should be at least reasonably unspoiled, that it should not be overburdened with commercial traffic—these two, of course, usually

go together—and that there should be suitable rivers, harbours, or sheltered anchorages where he can lie overnight
on, say, a short week-end cruise (most of us perforce do most
of our sailing at week-ends); and, lastly, that there should be
reasonable facilities for maintenance and repair, which in
most cases will mean a yacht yard of some sort.

You may just possibly live in a part of the country which
gives you a choice of sailing grounds. If you live in Central
London, for example, you will be more or less equidistant
from two large and famous yachting areas, namely the Solent
and the Thames Estuary. Only a minority of sailing men
will be thus strategically placed, however, and for most there
will be only one suitable stretch of coast within practicable
reach.

Anyway, whether you are able to choose your sailing
ground, or whether it chooses you, you would be well advised,
before buying your boat, to think a bit about its general
characteristics, and what sort of sailing you are likely to be
doing most of the time.

The important things to consider are the general topography of the area, and in particular the depth of water.
Small cruising yachts, especially those of recent design, are
of very moderate draught, but some still draw more than
others, and if your cruising ground is a shoal-water area,
with, perhaps, numerous creeks and rivers which you are
going to want to explore as thoroughly as possible (the
Thames Estuary is such an area), then draught will be important, and you may even decide that you would be wise
to buy a boat which has been specially designed for such
waters. If, on the other hand, 'ditch crawling' doesn't particularly appeal to you, and you feel that you will be content
to keep for the most part at any rate to the navigable channels in the area, and the open sea, then draught will not
matter so much (in a deep-water area it will naturally
matter even less, though there are surprisingly few such areas
around our coasts).

A five-ton yacht, which is as big a craft as you are likely to start off with, probably won't draw more than about four feet six inches, and this, so long as you are careful about your tides, will allow you considerable freedom of movement even in a shoal area. However, a word or two about craft which have been specifically designed for shoal waters may not be out of place here.

Some of these shoal-draught craft have centreboards, though this type is not greatly in favour nowadays. Quite a number of contemporary boats, especially some of the smallest ones, have twin bilge keels, which have the double advantage of reducing draught and enabling the boat to sit upright when she takes the ground. Just how much of an

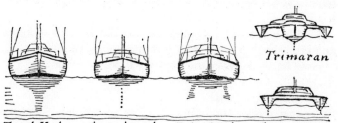

Fixed Keel   Centreboard   Bilge Keels   Catamaran

asset the latter can be will become apparent the first time the tide falls away and leaves you stuck on the mud for an hour or two.

An excellent example of a miniature twin-bilge-keel boat is the little two-berth Silhouette class, which has become very popular in recent years. Somewhat bigger, at four and a half or five tons, is the sturdy and seamanlike Westerly, while a prime example of a larger yacht in which the problem of draught has been overcome in a highly successful and original way is the Uffa Fox-designed Atalanta, which has twin retractable keels which are raised and lowered hydraulically. These yachts draw six feet with the keels fully down but only one foot six inches with them raised, which makes them equally suitable for either ditch crawling or sailing offshore.

Then again there are the multi-hulled craft, the cata-
marans and trimarans, which are now appearing in increasing numbers on the cruising scene. These craft, in addition
to their other advantages of speed and spacious accommodation, are also of very shallow draught.

Shoal-draught craft have another advantage, namely that
they can leave, get back to, and lie comfortably on, moorings
in shallower water than their fixed-keel sisters, which in turn
means that these moorings can be that much the more sheltered and nearer the shore. The latter can be quite a consideration in a shoal anchorage where boats of even quite
moderate draught have to lie some distance off if they are to
remain afloat at all states of the tide, necessitating a longish
trip in the dinghy.

Finally it should be emphasised that the properly designed
and built shoal-draught craft is thoroughly seaworthy.

Now let us consider the next question, which is:

(2) *How big a boat?*

Of course, money comes into this, but we will leave that uncomfortable factor aside for the time being and concentrate
simply on size. How big a boat should you start off with?

This will depend basically upon how many people will
normally be sailing with you, and also how big they are. A
lot of people take up cruising before they have families, in
which cases the normal complement of the craft will be two.
And the majority of people coming to cruising for the first
time will automatically think in terms of something very
small.

The smallest practicable cruising boats are of about two
and a half tons, which will probably mean two berths and an
over-all length of some eighteen feet. Such boats are not much
bigger than many dinghies, and the more modern of them
will have something of the same liveliness too. The ex-dinghy
man should be quite at home sailing such a boat. But he will
find living aboard her a bit cramped—especially on that
fortnight's summer cruise!

A lot of people start off with very small boats because they think they will be easier to handle than something bigger. This is not true. A five-ton yacht (which will be about twenty-five feet over all) with a modern sloop rig will be just as manageable and a lot more comfortable—more comforting, too, when a bit of weather comes along. I can vouch for this out of my own experience. I started cruising in a two-and-a-half-ton Hillyard, which was a marvellous little boat, but a *little* boat none the less, and when I graduated to a five-ton Vertue the change was fantastic, both as regards the comfort she afforded and the confidence she gave me. One might even say that the larger boat of the two is more manageable than the other. She will naturally be more stable, will give you more time to go about your handling of her, will stand up to the weather better, and will even look after herself as well as you when you make some of your inevitable mistakes, in a way that the smaller craft could not be expected to do.

It is scarcely necessary to point out that the bigger boat will almost certainly have more room below decks, but it may be worth emphasising that you can't really have too much of this. Most five-tonners have three or four berths—those built in recent years will almost certainly have four—and even if there are only two of you aboard, an extra berth or two will be a blessing, if only because it won't then be absolutely incumbent upon you to stow all your night gear away before the boat can be inhabited by day. And, of course, there will always be those occasions when you will want to take one or two other people with you.

If you have a family or friends who will be sailing with you regularly it is most desirable that you should have enough berths to go round. It's all very well to say that someone (not you) can sleep on the cabin sole, or draped round the toilet in the fore-peak. Reasonably comfortable sleeping quarters are, to my mind at any rate, a basic necessity of cruising. It can be a rough and tough game at times, and one person aboard in a bad humour because he didn't get his sleep can completely spoil everybody else's enjoyment. You are all at very close quarters in a small yacht, and tempers are important!

One thing you are unlikely to get even in a five-tonner is standing headroom below decks, except perhaps in the doghouse (the raised after-part of the cabin roof which some yachts have). To achieve this you normally have to go up to seven or eight tons, which is perhaps getting a bit big for a first boat, if only from the point of view of expense.

My advice, based on my own experience, would be to start off with a five-tonner, presuming that you can afford to do so.

Another point arises which may be of interest to anyone used to dinghy sailing. A five-tonner, and some even smaller cruising yachts, will be slower in her responses than the little cockleshell you have been sailing; some, particularly some older ones, can be frustratingly so. Modern boats tend to be a good deal nippier, and a five-tonner which is excellent in this respect is the now ubiquitous Folkboat. These little yachts, which are quite reasonably priced—and which *look* like yachts, which some modern designs do not, are very lively for their size. To start cruising in a Folkboat would seem to me to be an excellent thing for an ex-dinghy sailor to do, and I have in fact met a number of people who have done this, to their great satisfaction.

Now let us turn our attention to the third of the questions posed earlier:

(3) *New or second-hand?*

We shall frequently be stating the obvious in this book, because it is, after all, meant to be a 'first reader' in its subject, and I believe that some things can't be put too plainly. In any case even the obvious can have some unexpected or unconsidered aspects.

Fundamentally, whether you buy a new boat or a second-hand one will depend upon how big a boat you want, or must have, and how much money you have available. Broadly

Outward bound! The author's Vertue class yacht leaving harbour
at the start of a fortnight's summer cruise

Westerly 25 – a popular little
bilge-keel yacht

Westerly 22 – a smaller sister of the 25

(Reproduced by permission of Westerly Marine Construction Ltd.)

A Westerly 22 on her trailer

speaking you will get more boat for your money if you buy second-hand, though this doesn't necessarily mean that you will get more accommodation.

If you are one of the very few to whom expense is no object, then a wide choice lies before you. You could even have a boat designed and built to suit your own particular requirements, though I doubt whether this would be very wise for the beginner, since you can scarcely know what your cruising requirements are until you've had some direct experience. You can, of course, get a lot of good advice from yacht designers and builders, and a lot more, some of it perhaps less good, from other cruising men, but none of this would be as valuable as personal experience, not only of cruising but of ownership too, since the owner has a lot of things to think about which don't worry the 'crew' at all.

To have a first cruising boat built to your own personal requirements is therefore rather an extreme thing to do, and it must happen so rarely that we need not devote any further space to it here. What I would advise the beginner to do is to familiarise himself with the various types of yachts in his size which have been built to established and successful designs and go, if he can, for the one that suits his needs and pocket best. (Anyone who is seriously thinking of taking up cruising will doubtless get to know as much as he can, by reading the yachting journals, contacting designers, builders, and brokers, perhaps, and talking to other yachtsmen, about the kinds of craft which are available in his size and price range.) It is not essential that a yacht should have come from the board of a well-known designer, or have been built by a first-class yard, though these are useful guarantees that if there is anything wrong with your boat and her performance, it will probably be you.

It is, again, a rather unusual thing for the newcomer to cruising to have a yacht specially built even to an established design, for two reasons. One is that, as we have said before, he is unlikely to have enough knowledge or experience to be

B

absolutely sure what he wants, and any first boat must therefore be more or less a trial craft.

Secondly, as far as the smaller established classes of cruiser
are concerned, it is almost certain that enough of these will
have been built for there to be one or more on offer on the
second-hand market.

I would say, therefore, that the wisest course for anyone
to whom money is no great problem would be to buy a craft
of an established and reasonably recent design in as new
condition as possible.

For many people, however—indeed, for most—money
will be a very definite consideration, and some may find it
necessary to buy a considerably older boat to get the size,
etc., that they need.

An important point to be borne in mind here is accommodation—which is why I have added the qualification 'reasonably recent design' in the paragraph before last. Broadly
speaking, modern boats are roomier than old ones. There
has in fact been a revolution in this respect too since the last
war, and particularly in recent years. Many present-day five-
tonners have accommodation as good as or better than some
of the seven- or eight-tonners or even larger craft which
were built before the war. This really is something to think
about before you go rushing off to look at a boat which may
seem big enough over all but which may turn out to be disappointing and impracticable below decks.

Again I can speak from personal experience. Some years
ago there came on the market a veteran eight-tonner which
had belonged to a very distinguished sailor whom I had the
honour of serving under in the Royal Navy during the last
war. I was 'between boats' at the time, and in a sentimental
mood I went to look at her. I was glad I did, because she was
beautiful. But she was terribly poky below, with far less room
in her than the five-ton post-war Vertue which I eventually
bought—and Vertues aren't the most spacious of yachts
either.

Incidentally, you can spend a lot of time and money going

to look at boats, so it is desirable that you shouldn't make too many mistakes in this direction.

How old can a yacht be and still be a worth-while proposition? The broad answer is that it doesn't matter much so long as she is sound. There are yachts sailing today which were built at the beginning of the century, or even at the end of the last one. But, of course, the older she is, the more careful you must be to make sure she *is* sound.

One drawback with an old boat, apart from the question of accommodation, is that her gear may be heavy, unless

Gaff Rig   *Bermudan Rig*

she has been modernised in this respect. Actually in many cases this will have been done. For example, most of the oldest boats afloat today will originally have been gaff-rigged (gaff-rig, in its simplest form, means having a four-sided mainsail with a spar at the top). Very few yachts are built with this rig today, and many which were originally gaff-rigged have been converted to carry the simpler and more easily handled triangular Bermudan mainsail.

How do you assess the condition of a second-hand yacht? The answer here is that you can't, or you shouldn't, without help. If a yacht is not new, only an expert will be able to

make a precise assessment of her condition. Before buying
such a yacht, therefore, you should always have her expertly
surveyed.

Surveys

You should always have a second-hand yacht surveyed, unless a *very recent* survey report is available, preferably one
made after she was last used. To my mind this is essential
even if she is only a year or two old and to all appearances in
as-new condition. The fact is that you just cannot know
otherwise what has happened to her. She may, for instance,
if she is of wooden construction, have been banged down on
something hard and cracked a rib or two. And, as we have
indicated already, the older a boat is, the more vital a thorough survey becomes. I do know one man who bought a
fifty-year-old eleven-tonner without calling in a surveyor,
but he was an experienced yachtsman and, moreover, his job
was in wood, so in a sense he was his own expert. Even then,
if I had been he, I would have called in a professional. Certainly, for the ordinary person, buying a second-hand yacht
without a survey is a very foolish thing to do.

Getting hold of a surveyor is easy enough. Many of them
advertise in the yachting press. Alternatively the yard where
the yacht is lying, or the broker, if one is involved in the sale,
will put you on to a suitable man.

What does a survey cost? This will depend chiefly upon
the size of the craft. For a five-tonner the fee at the time of
writing is somewhere in the region of ten guineas. You may
have to add on to this the surveyor's travelling expenses, and
incidental expenses such as the yacht yard's charge for having
the yacht, if she is afloat, hauled out for the survey. No yacht
can be properly surveyed afloat, and no reputable surveyor
will attempt to do so.

Having a five-tonner surveyed may therefore cost you £20
or so altogether, and if, after that, you don't buy the boat, it
may seem a large outlay, especially since you are going to
have to fork out as much again next time. On the other hand,

taking into consideration the amount you would have paid for the boat, such a sum is well worth paying as insurance that you are not being sold a craft with serious and even dangerous defects.

The procedure when buying a second-hand yacht is to make an offer 'subject to survey'. Remember that the price quoted initially will be the asking price, and that it will usually—though not always—be possible to come down on this. Sometimes the price quoted will be qualified by the phrase 'or near offer' (o.n.o.), which means that you will certainly be able to get away with a bit less.

Presuming that the yacht is not in perfect condition—and very few are—the survey report should indicate two kinds of defect, firstly those which must be put right before the yacht can be considered seaworthy, and secondly those which should be attended to, perhaps in the fullness of time, but which will not affect the boat's basic safety or performance. It should be possible to estimate, from the information given in the survey, how much it will cost to have the yacht restored to a seaworthy condition, and it then only remains for you to add the cost of these repairs, and perhaps replacements such as sails and rigging, to the price you have offered, and decide whether you have got a good buy or not. If the price now seems excessive you may, especially if the defects are many or serious, be able to come to some arrangement with the present owner to cover them, at least in part.

There are various ways of finding a second-hand yacht. If you live in or near a yachting area you may come across what you want without, so to speak, really trying. Others not quite so favourably placed may choose to tour the yacht yards within reasonable reach of their homes, perhaps after briefing themselves from the ads in the yachting journals. Others, again, will find it more practicable to pick out from the ads a yacht of particular interest and make a special journey to look at her. In such a case it is only common sense to obtain permission to view before starting out, to avoid difficulties on the spot, or even an entirely fruitless excursion if the craft happens to have been sold since the ad was inserted.

You should also try to make as sure as possible that the yacht you have spotted in the ads is the sort of boat you really want, since a lot of time and money can be spent on these viewing trips, to say nothing of the discouragement which may follow upon a number of disappointments. Small ads inserted by private owners don't usually tell you much, and it's as well to write or phone for more detailed information before going any further. In the case of craft offered by brokers, the latter will send you on request a reasonably full description of the yacht concerned. In either case it is a good idea to ask for a photograph.

It is also necessary to avoid falling in love with an unsuitable yacht. This is not as flippant as it sounds. Boats are not called 'she' for nothing, and it is quite easy to lose your head over a craft which, almost irresistibly attractive though she may be to you for one reason or another, is in fact quite unsuitable for your purposes.

One last caveat. The ideal yacht is so rare as to be virtually non-existent, so don't waste your financial and physical resources looking for her. A yacht which is satisfactory in most respects will probably be as near as you can get. When you have got some cruising experience behind you you can start looking for your next and better boat—but when you've got her she won't be perfect either!

But now, before you actually start looking around, we'd better devote a little space to how much you are likely to have to pay, and how, if you haven't got the full price in your pocket, you can raise the necessary wind to get you sailing as soon as possible.

2

How You Can Find the Money

THE market price of a given size of yacht will vary a great deal according to whether she is new or second-hand, the repute of her designer, the materials of which she is built, the standard of construction, the standing of the yacht yard which built her, the amount, nature, and quality of the gear and equipment that goes with her, and so on. The price factor is indeed so complicated and so variable that it is very difficult to give any useful figures here, and the reader can really only be advised to familiarise himself with the prices which are current at the time when he is wanting to buy a yacht, *and to take particular note of what he will be getting for his money.* This he can most conveniently do, in the first instance, by studying the many ads which appear in the yachting press for both new and second-hand craft. He can then approach brokers, builders, or owners to make a closer assessment.

As the roughest possible guide, at the time of writing a new two-and-a-half-tonner might cost you £500 and a good second-hand one £400; a new five-tonner might be any-thing from £1,000 to £2,000, and a good second-hand one £1,000 to £1,500. These prices are based on the ads in the current issue of a leading yachting journal.

It is most important to find out just what you will be getting for your money, not only as far as the quality and condition of the actual construction are concerned but also as regards gear and equipment—in other words, how *complete* the craft is. You may, for example, see a new yacht advertised at what seems to you to be an extraordinarily low price, only to find on further investigation that she is 'ex-this' and 'ex-that' (ex-engine, ex-sails, and so on). The 'ex' simply means that these items are extra to the basic advertised price, and the unwary purchaser may find himself faced with having to spend almost as much again before such a craft is ready for sea. I can give you an instance of this. I recently looked at a new class of five-tonner for which the price asked was extremely reasonable, only to find that, by the time one had paid over the odds for the many essential or near-essential items which were not included, the price would have very nearly doubled, and she would have been a very expensive boat indeed. The uninitiated are often very surprised at how little a basic hull costs compared with the 'fixtures and fittings', and it is obviously desirable that this surprise should come before rather than after you reach for your cheque-book.

The above only applies, of course, to new craft. A second-hand yacht will probably be more or less complete, and in this case the extent and value of her equipment are an important factor. Prospective yacht purchasers are often puzzled as to why the price asked for a yacht which is two or three years old, or even older, is sometimes as high as or even higher than that of a new boat of the same design and construction. The answer will again most probably lie in these same fixtures and fittings. If the second-hand yacht has an extensive inventory of high-quality equipment—including, perhaps, an elaborate wardrobe of sails and a number of expensive aids to navigation—then these items may more than balance the amount by which she can be estimated to have depreciated from her new and 'basic' price.

Before you even begin to look at the 'craft for sale' ads at all seriously, however, you may want to get some idea of how much you can afford to pay for a yacht. Could you, for example, possibly run to that nice little five-tonner which has caught your eye?

As with most things, the amount you can afford to pay may depend upon how you pay. And there are three chief ways of buying a yacht. You can, of course, pay cash (perhaps with a loan from the bank). Secondly, you can do it by hire-purchase. Thirdly, you can, in some cases, do it on a mortgage.

It is pretty safe to say that those who can pay cash for any except the smallest cruising yacht are in the minority, the fortunate few. If you are thinking of buying a craft of any size at all—say a second-hand five-tonner—you are almost certainly going to have to spend £1,000, and probably a good deal more. And though most of the finance houses which deal in yacht purchase go in for a snobbish little euphemism about the advantages of buying your boat 'out of income, without disturbing investments', both they and we know quite well that most of us couldn't do it any other way—i.e. on deferred terms.

Paying cash outright is naturally the simplest and in the long run the cheapest way of buying anything, including yachts, and if you are in this privileged position you won't need any further advice on this subject from me. Nor do I propose to go at all exhaustively into the mechanics of buying a boat on deferred terms, since the prospective purchaser can easily contact one or more of the finance houses which deal with this sort of thing, to get their precise proposals. This he will have to do sooner or later anyway, either directly or indirectly, if he is going to buy a yacht in this way. At the same time a few pointers may be useful.

Yacht-purchase on deferred terms
Deferred terms can be arranged either direct with a finance house which undertakes this kind of business, or through the builders of the yacht, if she is new, or through the yard or

the brokers offering her for sale. If you are going to do it
through the builders or the yacht yard or the broker you
may not be able to choose which finance house you deal with.
If, on the other hand, you are going to make your own
arrangements with a finance house direct, then it isn't a bad
idea to 'shop around' and approach several of these companies, since their terms may vary quite a bit. Even if you
have been warmly recommended to one such company, perhaps by someone who has bought or is buying his own yacht
through that particular firm, it is still advisable to contact
others too, since you may find one that will suit your own
requirements better.

Most if not all of these finance houses advertise in the
yachting press, and a brief letter or phone call will bring you
all the necessary details.

Valuation. If you are going to buy a new boat on deferred
terms the finance company concerned will want the builder's
specification (and perhaps invoice) as evidence of the value
of the craft. If the boat is second-hand the company will
require, usually on all boats priced at more than £250, an
up-to-date survey report and valuation by an approved surveyor, on which to base their proposal. You may be able to
get away with an existing survey report, but it will have to
be a very recent one—usually one carried out within the
past three months. This means that you will almost certainly
have to stand the cost of a survey before you can proceed,
but since, as we have seen earlier, you would be very foolish
to buy a second-hand craft without having her surveyed,
this is no hardship.

Insurance. Comprehensive and third-party insurance
must be taken out on any craft, either new or second-hand,
before it can be bought on deferred terms. The finance house
you are dealing with will be happy to arrange this for you.

Hire-purchase—or mortgage? The essential difference

here is that mortgage terms are more favourable than those offered under a hire-purchase agreement. The period over which repayments can be spread may be longer, the rate of interest lower, and income-tax relief is allowable on the interest paid (you should receive from the finance house an annual certificate of interest paid to enable you to claim this relief).

There is a snag, however, and this is that a mortgage can be obtained only on a registered yacht, i.e. one which has been surveyed by an official surveyor of the Ministry of Transport and registered under the relevant part of the Shipping Act of 1894. If the craft you have in mind is unregistered you may wish to register her to obtain the more favourable mortgage terms, but this may not be a good idea either practically or financially. It depends upon the craft in question, and will need a particular inquiry with reference to her.

Down-payments and repayments

The amount a finance company will advance on either a mortgage or a hire-purchase agreement will depend largely on the valuation of the yacht. On a new yacht, or one in first-class condition, some companies will advance as much as four-fifths of the purchase price. As regards the interest payable on the amount advanced, there may be a considerable difference between that required on a hire-purchase agreement and the rate quoted for a mortgage, the latter being the lower. Both rates of interest may, of course, also vary from one time to another, but I have before me as I write this, a brochure from a finance house which points the difference. This company is currently asking, on a hire-purchase agreement, 8 per cent per annum flat on the balance of the price on new craft, and 9 per cent per annum flat on second-hand craft, while the interest payable on a mortgage on new and used craft is quoted at $5\frac{1}{2}$ per cent per annum flat.

'Flat' in the above means that the rate of interest quoted is that to be paid per annum on the amount borrowed at the outset, and not the amount outstanding in the year concerned. This means that on a three-year mortgage agreement at $5\frac{1}{2}$ per cent per annum you will have to pay a total of $16\frac{1}{2}$ per cent interest on the amount borrowed, and a correspondingly higher total percentage on a hire-purchase agreement. The difference can be considerable. Remember, too, that the mortgage terms are even more favourable than the figures just given indicate because, as we have mentioned already, income tax is recoverable on the interest paid. Also, a mortgage may make things easier in that, if you buy a boat in this way, you may be able to spread your repayments over as many as five years, whereas on a hire-purchase agreement the repayment period is more likely to be three years.

Incidentally, mortgage terms are negotiable between the finance house and the purchaser, whereas hire-purchase rates are governed by the current edicts of the Board of Trade.

Perhaps some actual figures, though they cannot be taken as anything but the roughest guide, will serve to clarify the above a little.

Hire-purchase and mortgage terms compared
To establish a unit of reference, let us compare the down-payments and instalment repayments one might have to make on a craft costing £1,000 (a) on hire-purchase if the craft were new, (b) on hire-purchase if she were second-hand, and (c) on mortgage if she were either new or second-hand (the rate of interest being the same on a mortgage agreement). To simplify the comparison we will assume that the down-payment required in each case will be one quarter (25 per cent) of the purchase price, and that the repayment period is in each case three years (remembering that on a mortgage it may be longer).

    (a) *£1,000 yacht, new, on hire-purchase*
       Down-payment of 25 per cent   £250
       Balance borrowed   £750
       Interest on balance at 8 per cent flat   £180

Total amount to be repaid   £930
Monthly instalment (36)   £25.16.8.

(b) *£1,000 yacht, second-hand, on hire-purchase*
Down-payment of 25 per cent   £250
Balance borrowed   £750
Interest on balance at 9 per cent flat   £202.10.0.
Total amount to be repaid   £952.10.0.
Monthly instalment (36)   £26.9.2.

(c) *£1,000 yacht, new or second-hand, on mortgage*
Down-payment of 25 per cent   £250
Balance borrowed   £750
Interest on balance at $5\frac{1}{2}$ per cent   £123.15.0.
Total amount to be repaid   £873.15.0.
Monthly instalment (36)   £24.5.5.

N.B. Under all the above arrangements, repayments can usually be made quarterly, if this suits you better.

There is one other most important thing to be borne in mind by anyone who is thinking of buying a yacht, and this is that your outlay won't by any means end with the buying of the yacht itself. You may be let in for a certain amount of further initial expenditure, and thereafter there will be maintenance, etc., to pay for.

Additional initial outlay
We have already dealt with the virtually unavoidable expense of having a boat surveyed (unless she is new; and we have seen that, once you have bought your boat, you may, if she is second-hand, have to spend some money on her before she is fit for sea). You may be able to get the previous owner to meet you on this, but it's unlikely that you won't have to find any of this money yourself.

If the yacht you buy is lying some distance away from the area in which you will be sailing her, and either (a) she is too big for you to transport on a trailer, or (b) you lack the experience, confidence, capable friends, or time to sail her home, you may have to have her delivered, either by sea or overland. This is arranged easily enough—the ad columns of the yachting press will help here too—but yacht delivery is apt to be a pricey business. Here it is impossible to provide any useful yardstick because so many factors are involved. Sometimes it will be preferable to have her delivered by road instead of by sea, but again, even if the distance is comparatively short, the bill is likely to be quite big.

Your additional initial expenditure may also include 'accessories' of various kinds, and some of these can be expensive too. You may, for example, have to buy a dinghy to use as a tender—after all, a yacht isn't much use if you can't get on or off her. Unless you are very lucky a dinghy isn't going to cost you less than £20, and it may cost a good deal more.

Then, when you've got your dinghy, what about an outboard to propel it? I personally prefer a pair of oars as being cheaper, healthier, as well as a lot less smelly and a good deal easier to stow. But if you are too lazy or too impatient to row, or if your yacht is lying on a mooring so far from your point of embarkation that mechanical motive power is a practical necessity for you to get out to her and back without too much waste of time and effort, then you are going to have to write another cheque. (At the time of writing, the smallest and cheapest outboards on the market are somewhere in the region of £30.)

There may also be clothing to be bought. And bedding. And charts. . . . The list can sometimes seem endless.

It is essential to both your comfort and your safety that you should start off 'well-found'. And it is important, therefore, from the point of view of your pocket, that you should take careful note of the quantity and quality of the gear, etc., which goes with the yacht you are thinking of buying. The better equipped she is already, the smaller your additional initial outlay will need to be. This is yet another truism, but it is extraordinary how many prospective purchasers don't realise the value represented by a yacht's inventory.

In the foregoing we have been concerned only with those items which are necessary. In the fullness of time you may feel—indeed, you almost certainly will—that you must acquire other items to improve your yacht's performance or add to your comfort, efficiency aboard, and so on. You may, for example, want to add to her sail wardrobe, or buy a depth recorder because you can't be bothered to go on using a lead line. Many of these items may be expensive, but, since they aren't basically essential, they don't really belong here.

Recurring expenses
These will be with you for as long as you own a boat, and many of them will recur every year. They include such things as :

Mooring charges
These are still very reasonable, except in some of the 'marinas' which have been springing up in increasing numbers in recent years, where they may be a considerable burden. The charge for an ordinary mooring ranges from a few pounds a year up to about a pound a week.

The difficulty with moorings is not so much their cost as their scarcity. With the great increase in popularity of cruising, moorings have become more and more difficult to obtain, with long waiting lists in many of the more popular yachting centres. So you had better make sure, even before you buy your yacht, that you have got or can get a mooring for her. Occasionally, but not often, a mooring will be offered with a yacht, and this is worth thinking about, unless the mooring in question is impracticably far away from home.

There are also a few ads for moorings in the yachting papers, but before renting one of these you should investigate it thoroughly, to see that it is really suitable for your yacht. You may find all sorts of snags. You won't, for instance, be very happy if you get stuck with one where your boat will lie afloat for only an hour or two either side of high water. And, of course, the deeper your boat's draught, the more careful about this you should be.

Yacht yard charges

You are unlikely to be able to do without the assistance of some kind of boat yard, particularly if you have a yacht of any size, and most of the expenditure you incur here will be recurring. You will probably have two regular bills to meet —for winter storage and for maintenance. Storage charges, like mooring charges, are usually reasonable, though on top of this you will have to pay to have your boat hauled out at the end of the season and put back in again at the beginning of the next. As far as yacht-yard maintenance is concerned, we shall be having more to say about this in a later chapter, but, briefly, your outlay here will depend very much upon how much of the work you do yourself and how much you get the yard to do. Few yachtsmen are expert enough, or have the time to spare, to do all their maintenance themselves, but many do as much as they can, and keep yard work to a minimum (generally speaking, yacht yards have no objection to yachtsmen doing their own maintenance, though it may be a good idea to give them a few jobs to keep them sweet). If you have your yacht wholly yard-maintained she will probably be kept in fine shape and look very nice— and the yard will be very nice to you too—but you will almost certainly get an alarmingly big bill.

Renewals, etc.

There will also be other expenditures which occur less regularly. These include such things as the renewal of gear (sails and standing rigging are among the largest items here). There will be the cost of running and maintaining your auxiliary engine (and outboard?). And, while we are on the subject of engines, you may have to take into consideration the hidden, but none the less real, expense of travelling from and back to your home every time you sail. This may not be a big item, but it will still cost more than a week-end's gardening or a deck-chair on the lawn.

Once again the list can seem endless. But don't be daunted —not that you will be, if you've caught the cruising fever!

The author's Vertue on her mooring. All ship-shape on deck . . .

. . . and down below too

(*By courtesy of City Centre Dockyard, Glasgow*)

One of the most popular of all five-tonners – the Folkboat

In spite of everything, a good many people in very modest circumstances manage to own and sail cruising yachts, and so can you.

So far we have had a general look at cruising, and got some idea of the outgoings involved. In the next chapter we will take a look at a few types of small cruising yacht with a view to your making up your mind which will suit you best.

3

Cruising Yachts—Hulls

WHEN you first set eyes on a yacht which is up for sale what do you see?

Presuming that she is not brand-new, her appearance will probably be misleading, and quite possibly disappointing. For one thing, though she may be afloat and rigged and looking like a yacht, the chances are that she will be laid up ashore, without her spars and either stuck away in a shed or covered with a tarpaulin.

Secondly, any yacht other than a new one is almost certainly not going to be gleaming and immaculate. Most craft come on the market at the end of the season, by which time they may be looking pretty shabby, and one which has been laid up ashore for any considerable period will probably be even shabbier.

Don't take too much notice of appearances. The important thing, of course, is that she should be sound. It is comparatively easy to slap on a coat of paint or varnish, whereas structural failures and horrible things like rot and electrolysis are different matters altogether.

The converse is true too. A new coat of paint may cover a multitude of sins. In both cases this is where the surveyor comes in.

A minor point, but one worth bearing in mind, is that a yacht laid up ashore, and particularly one laid up under cover—i.e. under a roof—will look a lot bigger than she will do afloat. A five-tonner in a small shed can look huge—such a leviathan, in fact, that the newcomer to cruising may feel that he and the crew at his disposal (his long-suffering wife, perhaps) cannot hope to handle such a craft efficiently. Getting aboard and down below will do a lot to restore a proper sense of dimension.

Another point of interest to the man used to sailing dinghies will be the variations of hull shape in cruising yachts. So perhaps we can now take a quick look at some of the hulls which may be tucked away in those sheds or hidden under those tarpaulins :

Hull form

The general shape of a yacht's hull is commonly and conveniently described by four measurements. These are (1) her length at deck-level, which is known as her L.O.A., or Length Over All; (2) her waterline length, which is her L.W.L., or Load Waterline Length; (3) her beam, or maximum width; and (4) her draught, or maximum depth in the water. These dimensions provide a formula which is useful for ads and brief specifications, and are usually given in the above order. A five-tonner, for example, may be described as being 26 ft. $\times$ 20 ft. $\times$ 7 ft. $\times$ 4 ft, which means she is twenty-six feet long at deck-level, twenty feet long on the waterline, seven feet wide at her widest point, and four feet deep from the water-level to the lowest point of her keel.

In the case of a yacht with a centreboard or other form of adjustable keel, two figures may be given for her draught, one for the depth of water she will draw with her keel fully lowered, and the other with it fully raised.

The above measurements will give a general idea of a yacht's lines. They must obviously bear a basic relationship to each other, but, positing a fundamental boat-form, they may vary from one design to another, sometimes quite con-

siderably. These variations may occur as the idiosyncrasies
of individual owners or designers, or they may represent
general trends. Yachts built nowadays, for example, tend to

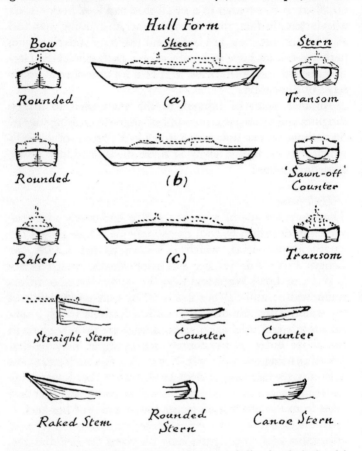

Hull Form

Bow	*Sheer*	*Stern*
Rounded	(a)	Transom
Rounded	(b)	'Sawn-off' Counter
Raked	(c)	Transom

Straight Stem   Counter   Counter

Raked Stem   Rounded Stern   Canoe Stern

be beamier, of shallower draught, and fuller in their 'ends'
than those dating from before the war.

The greatest variation is likely to occur in the difference
between a yacht's L.O.A. and L.W.L. This difference will
indicate her 'overhangs'—i.e. the extent to which her bow
and stern overhang the water. And these overhangs will

usually be a good guide to a yacht's age. Old yachts tend to have considerable overhangs, if they are 'true' yachts, and short or negligible ones if they were built on fishing-boat lines. In modern yachts the overhangs, generally speaking, are moderate.

These figures can tell us a good deal. An old yacht with little difference between her L.O.A. and her L.W.L. may be seaworthy and relatively comfortable, but she will almost certainly be heavy and slow. One with pronounced overhangs may be equally seaworthy, but she is unlikely to have what would nowadays be considered to be adequate accommodation for her size. She will probably be comparatively narrow in the beam, which means she will have long, sharp ends which are both difficult of access and far from ideal for either stowage or accommodation. She may also be a 'wet' boat too, since, with little fullness forward to give her buoyancy, she will tend to cut through the waves rather than ride over them.

As regards the actual shape of a yacht's ends, most craft on the market today will have a rounded bow form. Aft there is a greater variety of design. The old-style yacht usually had a counter stern, while more modern designs may have a modification of this (sometimes known as a 'sawn-off' counter), or a transom. The modified or sawn-off counter is usually found in craft rather larger than those with which we are primarily concerned here. For smaller yachts, and certainly for those of up to five tons, the transom stern is the most common. This provides more fullness aft and therefore more room for stowage, engine space, and cockpit accommodation.

In a few craft the stern is virtually a repetition of the bow. Such craft are known as 'canoe-sterned' or 'double-enders'. This design is almost exclusively Scandinavian and is not really desirable in very small yachts. Though it makes for seaworthiness, it has the disadvantage of reducing space aft.

The bow and stern profiles described above are illustrated on page 36.

The next most noticeable feature of a yacht's profile, or side-view, will be her sheer, which is the term used for the curve of her hull at deck-level. This will largely determine, at least for those who are conservatively minded (and who like a boat to 'look like a boat'), whether the hull is a pretty or an ugly one.

Examples of sheer are given on page 36. In (a) we see the profile of a hull which has a pronounced sheer, or a marked curve up towards the bows. This always makes a yacht look seaworthy. In some craft the sheer will be much less pronounced, and may in fact be flattened out completely (b). Some small modern yachts evince this characteristic. One of the main objects of such a design is to obtain more headroom below, and, pursuing this very desirable object, some designs go even further, so that we get a yacht with a 'reverse sheer', or humped profile (c).

From a utilitarian point of view, sheer is naturally more important in small yachts than in large ones, where headroom is not a problem and sweet lines can be achieved without reference to practical necessity. It is also to a large extent an aesthetic matter, a question of looks. If you aren't too bothered about graceful 'yacht' lines you may be willing to settle for the advantages of a boxier profile—the yacht won't necessarily sail any the less well. It all depends upon your personal preferences—or your pig-headed prejudices. For my own part, I would rather crawl about in a yacht with good lines than stand upright in one that looks like an expiring whale—even if she sails like a dream.

Now let us climb aboard and, before we do anything else, take a quick look at a yacht's deck-plan. This will normally be divisible into three main areas, namely the fore-deck, the 'midships or cabin area, and the after-part, most of which will probably be occupied by the cockpit.

Fore-deck
The chief features of the fore-deck will be :

A *samson post,* which is used when the yacht is lying at

anchor or on a mooring. This, as the name indicates, is a strong post; seated on the keel, it passes up through the fore-peak and protrudes through the fore-deck on the centre line a few feet from the bows of the yacht. It is used to secure the yacht when she is lying at anchor or on a mooring. The mooring or anchor chain will come inboard through a fair-lead on the stem, and will be turned up round the samson post. When the yacht is at anchor the slack of the anchor chain will then lead down through a hawse pipe or hole into the fore-peak. The inboard end of the anchor chain should always be secured in the fore-peak—for obvious reasons!

There may also be an *anchor winch* on the fore-deck, though this is not commonly fitted in yachts of the size we are discussing—i.e. of five tons and under. In yachts of this size the anchor can, in any but really abnormal conditions, be weighed by hand.

There will—or should—also be a chock stowage on the fore-deck to take the anchor when it is not in use.

Some yachts will have a *fore-hatch*, though this will not be normally found in the smallest types of cruising yacht. If the size of the yacht permits it, a fore-hatch is a desirable feature, provided that it is well constructed and watertight. Such a hatch will not only be a convenient means of access to the fore-part of the yacht, but will also greatly improve ventilation—always presuming that ventilation is desired, rather than the reverse!

A fore-hatch may be built into the fore-deck itself, or, in the case of a yacht with a cabin top extending forward of the mast (see below), into the forward end of the cabin top.

Cabin area

The major part of the 'midships section of a yacht's deck-plan will be occupied by the cabin top. In old, unmodified yachts this will probably be a one-level structure, raised a little above deck-level, with narrow side-decks to facilitate movement forward and aft. The cabin top will extend from the forward end of the cockpit to a little aft of the mast. In

more modern designs, or older yachts which have been re-
built in this respect, a number of modifications may have
been introduced. The after-part of the cabin top may be
raised to provide the doghouse which we have already mentioned, the cabin top may be extended forward of the mast,
and, thirdly, the mast itself may be stepped on deck instead
of passing through it. All these modifications have the same
object, namely to provide more, and more unrestricted, space
below decks.

A doghouse provides more room in what is in many cases
the working space below decks (we shall have more to say
about this later). It gives more headroom in that part of
the yacht and, with bigger ports than those in the cabin top,
lets in more light, which is a valuable consideration.

Doghouses are sometimes criticised as being necessarily
weaker in construction than the rest of the cabin top and,
because of their prominence, more vulnerable to a sea that
comes inboard, but, so long as they are well designed and
sturdily built, this is not really a factor to be taken into
account by the yachtsman who is going to spend his time in
modest coastal cruising. It is in fact true to say that a doghouse is an accepted feature nowadays of most yachts, whatever sort of sailing they may be doing. At the same time I
have seen some very flimsy ones, most of them later and
rather half-hearted additions to older craft.

A doghouse is also an important factor in the look of a
yacht. Well designed and constructed, it can be an asset
where appearances are concerned, but some are abomina-
tions. One that is too big—and particularly one that is
too high—can ruin the lines of an otherwise graceful
craft.

Another variation which is more likely to have been in-
corporated in the original design than to be a later modification is the cabin top which is carried right out to the sides of
the yacht, doing away with side-decks. Such a yacht is said
to have *raised topsides*. This is another way of increasing
the living space below decks, which it certainly does, and

again, if such a feature is well designed, the general lines of the yacht need not suffer.

The disadvantages of such a design can be two-fold. Some yachts with raised topsides are, to my mind at any rate, rather barn-like below—it's cosy to have a side-deck to tuck your shoulder under! This, I suppose, is a matter of opinion. Secondly, and less debatably, it is more difficult, with such a design, to move forward or aft on deck. You have to scramble

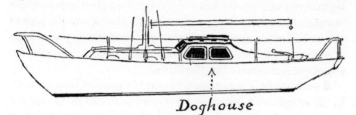

Doghouse

Raised Topsides

over the cabin top instead of being able to use one of the side-decks, with a hand-rail on the cabin top to hang on to.

Before we pass on to consider the third section of the deck-plan it may be worth just glancing at the question of dinghy stowage.

If you are contemplating anything at all of a passage, in anything like open water, you would be well advised to take your dinghy aboard if you can, however much of a chore this may seem at the time. Towing a dinghy can take a knot off your yacht's speed, and it will be one more thing for you to worry about in bad weather. As a cautionary tale in support of this, I can draw upon my own experience. I was running one day before a wind of about Force 6, with a steep following sea, when, looking astern to see if the dinghy was all right, I discovered that she wasn't there at all, and in fact was nowhere to be seen (I got her back later, virtually undamaged, through the excellent offices of my insurance people).

Whether you tow your dinghy or carry it on board will depend not only on the kind of passage you are about to make but also, of course, on the size of the dinghy and of the parent yacht. Generally speaking, it won't be possible or practicable to carry even the smallest conventionally built dinghy aboard a yacht of less than four or five tons.

If your yacht *is* big enough to take the smaller boat aboard, the most common stowage positions for it will be (a) on the fore-deck, where it will probably sit over the fore-hatch, if there is one; or (b) on the cabin top, provided that the boom of the mainsail is sufficiently high to clear it when it is in position there, and that the cabin top has sufficient unbroken length for the purpose (a doghouse can be an obstruction here). The dinghy, which will be carried inverted in either position, can be lashed in place, or, preferably, secured with gripes specially designed for the purpose. An inflatable or collapsible dinghy will naturally present less of a problem, and can either be stowed below or lashed on deck in some convenient position, such as on the cabin top.

There now remains the third section of the deck-plan to be considered :

After-part

In most yachts this space will be occupied by the cockpit, perhaps with an auxiliary engine under it, plus petrol tank and other stowage.

Take a good look at the cockpit. This can vary quite a bit in size even for a given tonnage, and its suitability in this respect for the sort of sailing you will be doing is, to my mind at least, something which ought to be taken into consideration when buying a yacht. Obviously the smaller the cockpit, the less vulnerable a yacht will be should the cockpit fill. But the less hospitable she will be too. If there are four of you aboard and there is only room for two—the helmsman and one other—in the cockpit, then you won't always have a very sociable time when you are under way. Sometimes the others will be able to dispose themselves about the decks, but British yachting weather doesn't encourage this very often, or at any rate not for very long periods at a time. Frequently some sort of protection will be required, and the best you will be able to manage in the above situation will be two in the cockpit, one on the bridge deck or in the cabin hatchway, and one below. It may be that you would prefer a cockpit large enough to take everyone on board, and for comparatively unadventurous coastal sailing this would not constitute an unwarrantable risk, since you would be very unlikely to encounter conditions in which the yacht would be in danger of being pooped or swamped.

A large number of yachts have self-draining cockpits— i.e. if the cockpit fills, the water is carried away through drain-pipes back into the sea. This is, of course, an excellent safety device, but again it is not one that must be considered essential in the above kind of sailing.

A few yachts have centre cockpits, in which case the accommodation will probably be split, with an after-cabin at the stern. In most such cases this will also mean that wheel steering will be necessary, or at any rate some kind of mechanical system, because of the distance between the rudder and the steering position. Centre cockpits are, however, rarely found in yachts of the size we are discussing here.

We have now had an 'outside' look at the hull of a yacht in both profile and plan. Perhaps this is a suitable time to consider very briefly the materials of which yacht hulls are commonly made :

Hull materials

The hull of a yacht will, with a few exceptions, be made of

one of three materials. It may, as in the case of sailing dinghies, be of wood, or of synthetic composition (fibreglass). The third material is steel.

Of these three, steel is rarely used for yachts of five tons or under, so this need not concern us any further here.

Fibreglass is a different matter altogether. There has been a great increase in the use of this material in recent years for the construction of yacht hulls, for reasons with which the dinghy sailor is probably already familiar. Fibreglass is light, extremely strong, impervious to rot and marine borers, and needs a minimum of maintenance. Such a hull will also be completely watertight, simply because there are no seams to leak.

The disadvantages of a plastic hull are—to repeat a word used earlier when we were discussing sheer—aesthetic rather than practical. Such a hull can *look* awful—like a bath-tub, or, particularly if the doghouse and cabin top are also of plastic material, like the product of some monstrous jelly mould. Also, the cheaper hulls are often left rough on the inside, so that one appears to be inhabiting a papier-mâché egg-box. There can, also, be an unpleasant coldness about such an interior.

The truth is that fibreglass is an unnatural and unsympathetic material, and is best when disguised by a judicious combination of fibreglass and wood. A yacht which has a plastic hull should be lined below decks at least in way of her living space, and if to this is added a laid deck, wooden cabin top, and cockpit coaming the result can be very attractive indeed.

The majority of yachts are still constructed of wood—which can't, if we are hard-headed about it, hold a candle to the new materials. Wood is not as strong as either steel or fibreglass. It is vulnerable to rot, electrolysis (the wasting caused by the electrolytic action set up by two unsuited metals in conjunction), and to the terrible teredo, the marine boring worm which can play such havoc with a wooden hull. It also requires a devil of a lot of maintenance. At the same time wood is a nice, boaty material, and a lot of yachtsmen are quite content with their wooden-hulled yachts. Many wouldn't have anything else. And some even *like* the hard labour of maintaining them!

Finally, before we leave the hull, we may as well glance at that very necessary appendage on the bottom of it, namely the ballast keel.

Ballast keel

We have already seen that some cruising yachts have centre-boards or some other form of retractable keel, while others have bilge keels. These, though, are in the minority. The majority will have a fixed ballast keel, mounted centrally on the fore-and-aft line of the hull.

The ballast keel performs the double function of acting as a righting lever and of providing part of the hull's resistance to leeway.

The best material for a ballast keel is lead, because of its great density—i.e. its heaviness for a given volume. But lead is so expensive nowadays that a lead keel is likely to be found only on an old yacht or on a pricey newer one. The ballast keels of most small yachts are made of cast iron.

The ballast keel is bolted on through the keel of the yacht itself. It is a major surveying point that one or more of these keel bolts should be drawn and examined for wastage, and this is in turn one of the chief reasons why a yacht cannot be satisfactorily surveyed afloat.

Bilge keels perform the same functions as the centrally mounted ballast keel, and so, to some extent, does the centre-board or retractable keel. In some yachts, whatever kind of keel they may have, but more particularly in the case of those with centreboards, an additional amount of interior ballast will be required. This normally takes the form of iron 'pigs' positioned in the bilges of the yacht. This interior ballast can be something of a nuisance in that it will be necessary to remove it from time to time for cleaning, but such an

46 TAKING UP CRUISING

arrangement has the minor advantage that the trim of the
yacht can be adjusted by moving the inside ballast.

So much for the shape and fabric of the hull. In the next
chapter we will consider the means by which this floating
container is propelled.

4

Cruising Yachts—Rigs and Engines

ONE difference between a sailing dinghy and a cruising yacht is that, whereas the dinghy will have only one means of propulsion (her sails), the yacht, at any rate if she is of any tonnage at all, will almost certainly have two. In addition to her sails she will have some form of auxiliary engine.

The word 'auxiliary' suggests that the engine will be a secondary source of power. Just how secondary it is, or should be, is something we will be discussing later in this chapter. First let us consider the means of propulsion a cruising yacht shares with a dinghy, namely her sails.

Another difference between a sailing dinghy and a cruising yacht is that, while dinghy rig is fairly standard, yacht rig can be more varied, this variation being to a large extent, though not entirely, connected with the size of the yacht concerned.

Virtually all dinghies, except those which have only one sail, are sloops. In other words, they have a single mast and a basic two-sail rig, the two sails being a mainsail and a fore-sail, or jib. A cruising yacht may have more than one mast, and a basic or 'working' rig consisting of more than two sails.

A cruising yacht may be a sloop, a cutter, a yawl, a ketch, or even a schooner, with certain variations within these categories as well, which are outside the compass of this book. The basic rigs listed above are given in declining order of incidence, and only the first really concerns us here. At the same time a brief note about each may be useful, if only for future reference.

Sloop rig

The majority of small cruising yachts afloat today are sloop-rigged, and this is a rig with which the dinghy sailor will be wholly familiar since it is identical with that which he has been used to.

A sloop-rigged craft, whether she is a dinghy or a larger yacht (she can be a great deal larger), will have a single mast stepped roughly a third of her over-all length from the bow, and her working canvas will consist of a mainsail and a foresail, or jib. This is the simplest form of yacht rig, and it is as efficient as any. Hence its popularity. It only becomes impractical in larger yachts, and then only in certain circumstances (see later).

Cutter rig

A yacht which is rigged as a cutter will have a single mast stepped rather further back than it would be in a sloop. A cutter's basic rig consists of a mainsail and two headsails, where the sloop has one. Cutter rig is a pretty rig, and a very seaworthy one, but it is not nearly so common as sloop rig, for the very good reason that for the ordinary and comparatively unambitious cruising man it offers no particular advantages over the simpler two-sail rig. Devotees sing its praises, and make much of the fact that, because the mainsail is carried further aft, it is easier to heave to in a cutter than in a sloop. This, however, will in practice largely depend upon the individual yacht—and the skill of those handling her. Nor is this a virtue which need concern us here, since very few coast-hopping cruising types ever meet conditions in which they would need to heave to—or would know how to if they did!

The remaining rigs are two-masted rigs. These are usually found in larger craft, and their main purpose is to break up the total area of working canvas into smaller and therefore more manageable sails than the same yacht would have

Rigs

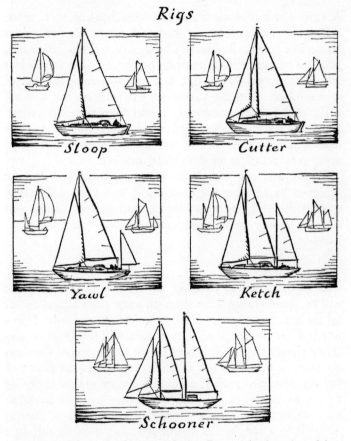

to carry with a single-masted rig. In particular the object of the two-masted rig is to avoid having to carry a very large mainsail. One of these rigs would be preferable, for example in the case of a large yacht which was normally under-manned or sailed by an elderly or not very robust crew.

D

Two-masted rigs also have the advantage that the total sail area can be reduced by the handing of individual sails instead of by reefing.

Yawl rig

A yawl has a mainmast and another, much shorter, mast, called the mizzen mast, stepped well aft (abaft the rudder post). The basic sail-plan will be that of a sloop (or cutter), plus the mizzen. This is another 'pretty' rig, and an efficient one, as is proved by the fact that an appreciable number of successful ocean-racing yachts are yawl-rigged. But it is not a rig that is very commonly found in very small yachts. Generally speaking, yawl rig is not justified in yachts of less than about six tons. Below this size the mizzen will be so small as to be little more than an affectation.

With yawl rig, an effective reduction of sail can be achieved by handing the mainsail. A true yawl will handle reasonably well under headsail(s) and mizzen alone, and this can be very useful, particularly when entering or leaving harbour.

Ketch rig

This rig is similar to yawl rig, except that the mizzen mast will be considerably taller than (in some cases almost as tall as) the mainmast, and will be stepped further forward (forward of the rudder post). The mizzen will therefore be correspondingly larger. This is not a rig for yachts of less than about eight tons. It is not as efficient to windward as any of the rigs discussed earlier, and, with the exception of one or two large yachts, is not used for racing. It offers the same advantages as yawl rig of permitting a reduction in the size of the largest sail carried and of reducing the total sail area by taking off individual sails instead of reefing.

Schooner rig

This is a two-masted rig in which the masts are comparatively close together and the mainmast and the taller is the one aft. This is not only a rig for large yachts but is also one which is rarely found in our waters, since it is not good for the windward work which is such a dominant feature of our yachting. It is much more common on the eastern seaboard of the United States, where beam winds are more often met with.

The foregoing are the main types of rig for yachts, but there is also a broad differentiation which is applied to them in general. All craft under sail can be classified as being either Bermudan-rigged or gaff-rigged, depending upon the shape of their mainsails.

The dinghy sailor will already be familiar with Bermudan rig, for the Bermudan sail is the triangular mainsail which he has been used to in his smaller craft. The Bermudan mainsail of a cruising yacht is likely to differ only in size, the weight of the material of which it is made, and possibly in the means by which it is attached to its spars. A gaff-rigged sail is a four-sided sail, the head of which is supported by a spar called the gaff—hence the name. This type of sail needs somewhat more complicated hoisting arrangements than the Bermudan sail, and it is not generally considered to be as efficient on the wind as the simpler triangle. For this reason it is rarely found nowadays except on yachts of a considerable age, and many old yachts which were originally gaff-rigged have been converted to Bermudan.

A yacht which has two masts may carry one of these four-sided sails on one of them and a Bermudan sail on the other, in which case she is sometimes described as being gaff-rigged on whichever mast it may be.

To sum up, by far the most common type of small yacht afloat today, from the point of view of rig, is the Bermudan sloop.

Now let us look at a yacht's complement of sails, which is commonly known as her 'wardrobe'. When buying a yacht, particularly a second-hand one, the number and condition of the sails included in the inventory should be carefully

taken into account since a considerable monetary value may
be represented here.

Sail wardrobe

For the sake of simplicity, let us assume that our yacht is a
sloop. We have already seen that in the great majority of
cases she will be.

The basic or 'working' canvas of such a craft will be precisely that of the average sailing dinghy, namely a mainsail
plus a foresail (which is sometimes called the jib).

This sail area may be *increased* by the addition of (a) a
larger foresail (a staysail, or Genoa), and (b) a spinnaker,
the balloon-type sail with which most dinghy sailors will
already be familiar.

Means must also exist for *reducing* the basic area of canvas carried, at the same time preserving the balance of the
sail plan. Where the mainsail is concerned, this will be done
by reefing. To achieve the necessary relative reduction of
sail area forward of the mast, the foresail may also in certain
cases be reefed, but a much more common practice nowadays
is to change the working foresail for a smaller one. A modern
five-tonner will probably carry a working foresail, or jib, and
two smaller ones, and these three sails will usually be de-
signated 'Number One', 'Number Two', and 'Number Three
Jib', in decreasing order of size.

With regard to reefing the mainsail, most yachts in com-
mission nowadays are equipped with roller-reefing gear,
although here and there a sail with the now old-fashioned
reef points will be found. Roller-reefing, with which most
dinghy sailors will already be familiar, and in which the sail
is rolled up on the boom like a blind, is preferable for the
reason that has governed so much of the progress in yacht
design—it is simpler, quicker, and easier to operate than any
other method yet discovered.

In the same way, most yachts now sailing have mainsails
which are attached to the mast by slides, just as is the case
with sailing dinghies, though just very occasionally, on old

yachts gaff-rigged on the main, mast-hoops, which attach the sail to the mast like curtain rings on a pole, will be found.

The foot of the mainsail may also be equipped with slides working along a track on the boom (this arrangement will be found aboard most small modern yachts of any calibre). Alternatively, the foot of the sail may be lashed to the boom —or it may, in one or two unusual instances, be 'free-footed'.

Yachts which make long sea passages may require to make a reduction of sail below the minimum noted above, and will carry a trysail and storm jib for this purpose, the trysail being a small but extremely tough triangular sail which is rigged in place of the completely furled mainsail. But the weather conditions necessitating this degree of sail reduction will not —we hope—come within the experience of the ordinary cruising man, and these sails will not form part of the wardrobe of the average short-cruising yacht.

Sail materials

The revolution now being brought about in the world of yachting by the introduction of synthetics is as great here as it is in hull construction. Nylon, terylene, and similar synthetic materials have very definitely 'arrived' where yacht sails are concerned.

The development of synthetic sails was inevitably accompanied by a number of teething troubles, but most of these have been successfully overcome and nowadays these sails have few disadvantages compared with the old 'cotton'. Virtually their only drawback in most yachtsmen's eyes is the fact that they are initially more expensive—but, against that, they last longer. And they have one great advantage which, from the point of view of the yachtsman who must be off and away from his yacht as soon as he gets back to his mooring, pretty well outweighs anything else. This is that synthetic sails can be stowed away wet without suffering any harm, whereas such a practice would soon ruin a cotton sail. This is a very great boon indeed to the yachtsman whose time is limited—and that means almost all of us.

Many small yachts of recent vintage will have synthetic sails. If you are buying a new craft you may have a choice of synthetic or cotton, the price being adjusted accordingly. Some older craft will have nothing but cotton, but the yacht which nowadays does not include at least one sail made from one of the new materials in her wardrobe is becoming increasingly rare.

Sail stowage

Sails should be stowed individually, preferably in sail bags specially made for the purpose, each bag being clearly marked in some way to indicate its contents. It is extremely frustrating to have to pull half a sail out of its bag before you can find out which one it is (and almost inevitably it will be the wrong one).

The sails will normally be stowed, in their sail bags, in the fore-peak, or in some cases aft, in the cockpit lockers. Fore-peak stowage is obviously preferable if the yacht has a fore-hatch, since it is usually the headsails which will be changed on passage. Fore-peak stowage will also in most cases be cleaner, or at any rate further removed from soiling by oil or grease from the engine.

One divergence from dinghy sailing practice may be noted here. A dinghy's mainsail will normally be removed at the end of each outing, whereas a cruising yacht's mainsail may be left stowed on the boom (preferably with a sail cover over it).

As we have said already, sails are an expensive item, and therefore an important element in the cost of maintenance. It is unlikely, however, that you will have to worry too much about this when you first take up cruising. The working life of any sail will depend to a large extent upon how much it is used, and in what conditions, but it is fairly safe to say that if a yacht's sails are in good condition when he buys his craft the newcomer to the game won't need to worry about them for several seasons to come. This is particularly true in the case of synthetic sails.

Now let us briefly consider the means by which a yacht's sails are supported and presented to the wind. Again, for the sake of simplicity, we will assume that the yacht is a sloop.

Spars

Until comparatively recently, almost all yacht spars were made of wood, either solid or hollow-section. Nowadays metal (light alloy) spars are becoming more and more common, and it looks as though glass fibre will soon be invading this field in strength too.

It is obvious from the foregoing that the older a yacht is, the more likely it will be that she will have wooden spars. And it is, I think, equally true to say that the *smaller* a new yacht is, the more likely it will be that she will have metal spars. Many modern dinghies have alloy masts, and it seems that, generally speaking, this particular change is spreading from the smallest sailing craft upwards.

Traditionalists, of whom there are probably more in yachting than in an other sport, are inclined to regard the introduction of metal spars in much the same way as they do the use of glass fibre for yacht hulls, and for much the same reason. The 'aesthetics' of the matter are again to the fore. A wooden yacht mast is often a thing of beauty, as well as being the product of the most skilful craftsmanship, compared with which the metal mast is apt to look like a length of piping stood on end. At the same time the metal mast will, or should be, stronger and lighter for a given height than its wooden counterpart, and will be both easier to maintain and less liable to deterioration.

The typical modern cruising sloop will have the same spars as a sailing dinghy. She will have a mast and a boom for her mainsail and, if her sail wardrobe includes a spinnaker, a lighter spar for this as well. Some older yachts have bowsprits, but with the modern tendency towards an 'all inboard' rig, these are rarely seen nowadays. Some yachts may have a bumkin (a sort of bowsprit-at-the-back) to carry a standing backstay clear of the mainsail (see page 56).

Rigging

Any sailing craft's rigging can be divided into two kinds—standing rigging and running rigging. As these two terms indicate, standing rigging is that which is set up more or less permanently to support the mast or masts, and sometimes certain other spars, while running rigging is, generally speaking, that by which the sails are hoisted and controlled.

Standing rigging

In this connection it is important to realise that a yacht's mast has of itself insufficient power to resist the forces which may be imposed upon it, and that therefore the strength and correct setting up of her standing rigging are vital.

Let us look at the standing rigging of a small cruising sloop :

A major part—in some cases almost all—of the necessary lateral support for the mast will be provided by shrouds, which will consist of one or more stays on either side of the mast.

The mast will be supported from forward by a fore-stay (from the bow of the yacht, preferably to the masthead). There may be another shorter stay from the bow to a point short of the top of the mast, on which the foresail, or jib, will be hoisted.

In some cases there will be a permanent stay from the top of the mast to the stern of the yacht (perhaps carried out by a bumkin to clear the mainsail). This is known as a 'standing backstay'. (Such a stay will not be possible with gaff rig, since it would obstruct the top of the mainsail, which with this rig rises above the top of the mast.)

On some yachts, diagonal support from aft will be provided by twin *runners*, stretching from a point near the top of the mast to positions on the port and starboard sides of the yacht towards the stern, usually roughly abreast of the cockpit. These runners are adjustable. When sailing, the weather or windward runner must be set up taut to provide support for the mast while the one to leeward is slacked off to prevent it obstructing the swing-off of the boom and the set of the mainsail. Some runners are equipped with setting-up levers, which are a great advantage. The runners have to be adjusted—one set up and the other slacked off—while the yacht is going about, and with levers this operation can be carried out quickly and correctly with a single simple movement of each lever.

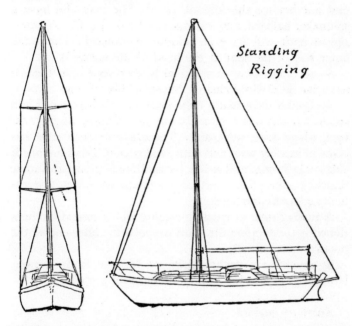

*Standing
Rigging*

Standing rigging is normally made of either galvanised or stainless-steel wire. The latter is the more expensive, and has the advantage of not being subject to corrosion. Some yachtsmen think that stainless-steel rigging can be dangerous in that it does not obviously betray its weaknesses, but this is a very debatable point.

When buying a second-hand yacht, particular attention should be paid to the condition of her standing rigging (any surveyor worth his salt will make a special point of this).

Upon this most important factor may depend nothing less than the safety of the yacht and those aboard her.

Running rigging

This consists basically of *halliards*, which hoist the sails, and *sheets*, which control their presentation to the wind.

A Bermudan sloop will have one halliard for the mainsail and another for the foresail, or jib. She may also have a spinnaker halliard, and a staysail halliard. A gaff- or gunter-rigged craft will have an additional halliard to hoist the outer end of the spar at the head of the mainsail.

Some yachts have wire halliards, with rope tails (there is less 'give' in a wire halliard). Sheets will be of rope.

Synthetics have made their presence felt here too. Until recently hemp was commonly used for running rigging (except where wire was used). Nowadays terylene rope has come in in a big way, and with good reason. Terylene rope is extremely strong, and it has the additional great advantage that it remains pliable and easy to handle when wet, whereas hemp goes stiff and hard.

A further item of running rigging which should be mentioned is the topping lift. This supports the after-end of the boom of the mainsail.

So much for a yacht's 'primary' form of motive power. Now let us look at her secondary means of propulsion.

Auxiliary engines

The first question to be asked here is : why, if our intention is to go cruising *under sail*, do we need an engine at all ?

The answer is simply that for most of us, whether we like it or not, time will be an essential factor in our cruising. To those bold, free souls who are able to go in for long ocean voyages, an auxiliary engine may well be more of a nuisance than it is worth, because the range of such an engine on the amount of fuel that can be reasonably carried will be negligible compared with the total distances involved, and the room taken up by such an engine and its fuel may be much

more valuable as stowage for other things. Nor do cruising
men of this calibre have to worry, at any rate within a day
or two, about when they make port. The rest of us, on the
other hand, will be sailing to a much tighter schedule. For
many of us, for example, the joyous sense of freedom and
release with which we embark on a week-end afloat will
be tempered by the thought that we must be back in time
to get to the office on Monday morning. We must, therefore,
whether we like it or not, have some means of propulsion
which is fundamentally independent of the elements. If we
are ten miles from home on Sunday evening when the breeze
finally fails, or we need to reach a certain point at a certain
time to catch a home-going tide, or even if we are a couple
of hundred yards from our mooring when the tide turns
foul and there isn't enough wind to overcome it, then a
'mechanical topsail' is our only way of keeping to our E.T.A.

Again, nowadays many yachting anchorages are so
crowded with craft that under any except the most favourable conditions of wind and tide, and sometimes not even
then, it is scarcely possible to leave or return to our mooring
under sail without taking unwarrantable risks, which may
well involve other yachts as well as our own. Under these
circumstances it is only sensible, and considerate, however
much it may hurt our sailorly pride, to leave and enter harbour under power, and most yachtsmen today make a habit
of doing this. Apart from the safety angle, motoring out and
in also saves a lot of time which can be spent much more
profitably and pleasurably at sea.

We may say, therefore, that for everyone except the die-
hards and the long-distance merchants, some degree of auxiliary power is a virtual necessity. The question then follows :
how much of this kind of power do we want? Do we want
the minimum, i.e. an engine which is just big enough to get
us out into the open and back again, and push us across a
flat patch or against a tide now and again; or do we want the
kind of performance under power which will match the best
we can do under sail?

This is a matter of choice, though if you buy a second-hand yacht the chances are that the choice will have already been made for you, and that the yacht will have a moderate performance under power. At the same time engines varying considerably in capacity can be found in yachts of a given size, within the range mentioned in the previous paragraph; that is, from the smallest possible unit to that which will match the best the sails can do (such a craft, incidentally, is commonly known as a motor-sailer, or a 'fifty-fifty').

So—what will suit you best? To my mind a fifty-fifty is not much more than a motor boat with sails, and, for me, having so much mechanical power to hand would destroy a lot of the point and take most of the fun out of getting anywhere under sail; but obviously not everyone thinks this way, or such craft would not exist. On the other hand, an engine which is so small that it barely gives you steerage way even in calm conditions can be very frustrating. The golden mean is an engine which will push your yacht along quite briskly without making you dissatisfied with her performance under sail. This, as we have indicated, is the sort of engine that most yachts have.

Next, what *sort* of engine should you have? Some of the smallest cruising yachts have to make do with outboards, but these are a nuisance in that some sort of stowage must be found for them when the yacht is under sail. Even when a specific stowage is provided, this may be unsatisfactory, or at the best space-consuming, and there will still remain the tedious business of shipping and unshipping the engine.

In any yacht in which its installation is practicable, an inboard engine is an infinitely better bet. Such an engine will be properly installed, normally under the cockpit, with controls coming through to the helmsman's hand, and will be an unobtrusive and integral part of the yacht.

Inboard engines can be divided into two main categories, namely petrol engines and diesel engines. What are the respective advantages and disadvantages of the two kinds? Personally I would plump for a diesel every time, provided that I could afford it. Diesel engines are, by and large, more expensive than petrol engines, and some of them are noisier, but this is about all that can be said against them. On the credit side they have two advantages which to my mind are of overwhelming importance. In the first place there is no fire risk, and secondly an engine without electrics is a great boon at sea. Salt water is death to electrical equipment, and the protection of the latter must therefore be a matter of constant concern.

One last, non-technical point with regard to engines: whatever size or type you have, it must be *reliable*. A lot of yachtsmen go to sea with engines which either won't start at all when they are wanted to, or which will only do so after the expenditure of a good deal of time and effort (and temper). Such engines are one of the standing jokes of yachting, but they are no joking matter really. To have an erratic engine is worse than to have none at all, if only because its failure, in a situation which reliance upon it has led you into, may result in difficulties, or even danger.

Provided that the engine is not irremediably decrepit, the answer here is maintenance. Too many yachtsmen regard their auxiliary engine as a rather unnecessary bit of machinery mercifully hidden away under the cockpit, and never, if they can help it, take any interest in it or give it any attention from the beginning of the yachting season to the end. The truth is that regular cleaning, maintenance and test-running are most necessary, the more so because the average yacht engine is poorly protected from its arch enemies of dirt and damp. It should be properly looked after, and no less reliable than the engine of your car.

5

Below Decks

COMFORT and facilities below decks are more important in a cruising yacht than in one which is primarily used for racing, not only because in most cases longer periods of time will be spent afloat but also because living aboard is, or to my mind should be, one of the pleasures of this kind of sailing. When racing, of course, the object is to get from here to there, and possibly back again, as quickly as possible, and racing yachts, even quite large ones, are often dauntingly spartan below.

The basic 'domestic' requirements of life afloat are the same as those of life on land. We need facilities for eating, sleeping, and performing our toilet. Let us examine these three requirements in this order.

Food—the galley

On any except very short trips, eating will mean cooking—and even on an afternoon's sail a cup of tea will probably be welcome at some stage in the proceedings!

Cooking means that the yacht must carry some sort of stove, and how big and elaborate this will be will depend on the amount of space available and on how well you want to do yourself and your crew. For example, you may consider

an oven an unnecessary refinement, even if you have room
for one. When I bought my five-tonner the inventory included a portable oven (a sort of tin box that you stuck on
top of the stove). Feeling that I and anyone who sailed
with me might reasonably be expected to exist for periods of
up to a fortnight without roast beef and so on, and that the

Below Decks

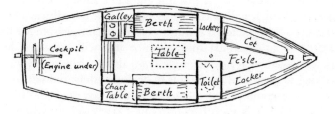

stowage space this article took up could be more profitably
used, I promptly flung the thing overboard, and never had
cause to regret doing so.

On the smallest yacht there will probably not be room
for more than a single primus, or one of the modern bottled-
gas equivalents. How well you eat will then depend to a
large extent on the cook, but you can still manage very satisfactorily—after all, there will almost certainly only be two of

you. At the other end of the size-range we are concerned
with, a five-tonner will very likely have a two-burner stove,
functioning on either paraffin or bottled gas.

Almost all yacht stoves burn one or the other of these two
fuels, and there can be no doubt that of the two the gas stove
is the more convenient. There is still some prejudice against
this kind of stove because of the possibility of a gas leakage
and the consequent danger of an explosion, but even with
a two-burner stove which has a 'remote' supply from a cylinder, and therefore a system which involves piping which may
be fractured, there need be no real risk of this. Care should,
of course, be taken to check from time to time that the piping
is in good condition, but the best precaution of all is to make
sure that the gas supply is turned off after every use *at the
cylinder*. This will make leakage impossible. Even a paraffin
stove, which some people feel happier with, has its hazards
if it is not used properly. You may, for instance, get a flare-
up, with the attendant danger of fire.

It is desirable that if possible the stove should be hung in
a frame which will permit it to swing with the athwartships
motion of the yacht (it is not necessary to compensate for the
factor of fore-and-aft motion since this will be much less
pronounced in terms of angle from the horizontal). Such a
device is essential if cooking is to be done safely and with any
degree of comfort and efficiency in even average conditions
at sea, and it is useful in harbour too, especially when, as
seems to happen only too frequently these days, a speed-boat
or some other power craft passes too close and too fast and
makes your floating home rock violently.

In most cases in which a device of this kind is fitted, it
will be possible to use the stove in two positions—either suspended, or sitting firmly on the surface below it.

What else do you need for your meals on board? Obviously you must have crockery and cutlery—and some food
would be a good idea too. Some yachts have specially designed stowages for crockery, or at any rate for cups and
glasses, and this is a great boon. It is, incidentally and for very

(*By courtesy of Lee-Wright Limited, subsidiary of Normand Electrical Company Limited*)

Sirius – an attractive new five-tonner now being built in the West Country

The Haward
Safety Harness –
quickly attached

(Reproduced by permission of P. J. Haward)

The Haward
Safety Harness –
easily adjusted

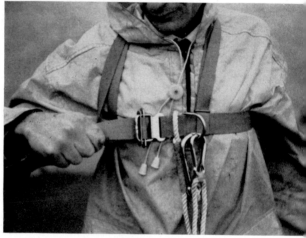

(Reproduced by permission of P. J. Haward)

(Reproduced by permission of P. J. Haward)

The Haward
Safety Harness –
can be clipped on
to any suitable
point

obvious reasons, a good idea to have crockery of some un-breakable kind. Actual stowage space for this and for food is not usually a problem. A good stowage for tinned food—and for beer and wine, etc., in cans too—is in the bilges under the cabin sole, where it will, so to speak, take up no room at all. A word of warning here, though : if you are wise you will remove the wrappers or labels from such cans as depend upon these for their identification and mark them in some other, more permanent way. Otherwise the bilge water may remove them for you, and then you may not be able to tell whether you are opening a can of baked beans or Beau-jolais.

While we are still on this subject, we may as well have a word about a chore that is always with us, ashore or afloat, namely washing up. A five-tonner may have a sink, but it is unlikely that you will find this amenity in anything very much smaller. Still, a sink is very much a luxury, really, aboard a boat, and a lot of people manage very happily with a bowl—which, incidentally, will no doubt also do duty for washing and shaving, etc., since very few yachts indeed in our range run to the refinement of a washbasin.

Again, while we are talking about food, what about a table? This is something of a problem since even a five-tonner can scarcely accommodate a centrally positioned table, even of a fold-down type, without it taking up a good deal of room in the cabin and obstructing passage fore and aft. Such a table may be portable, but you will find it a nuisance to have to erect and dismantle it, particularly if you are tired at the end of a trip—and, of course, stowage must be found for it when it is not in use. Various other fold-down or collapsible devices are employed, some of them very strange and difficult to use, and some of them all right as long as they do not collapse at the wrong time. In a very small boat, however, you may have to eat off your knees, or the bunk alongside you, or out in the cockpit if the weather is kind. In fact under reasonable conditions, and particularly in harbour, the cockpit will probably serve as both an extension of the 'kitchen' and as a dining room, which is another reason why it should not be too cramped and uncomfortable.

An essential which must be accommodated for both cooking and washing is fresh water. Some yachts towards the top end of our range may have a built-in tank for fresh water, with a tap to draw it off—my own five-tonner had a tank holding eighteen gallons. This kind of fresh-water storage is, of course, a blessing, especially if facilities exist at your home port for filling it from a hose, but many yachts have to store their water in containers. It is, however, surprising how little fresh water you can get along with, and the advent of polythene and similar substances has resulted in the appearance on the market of a wide range of containers which are both lighter, easier to stow and more convenient in almost every way than metal ones.

There remains the question of the position of the galley. Just occasionally, particularly in older and larger craft, this will be located in the forward part of the yacht, but it will much more frequently be found to port or starboard at the after end of the cabin. This, to my mind, is where it should be, especially if the yacht has a doghouse to provide additional light and ventilation. As far as our sort of cruising is concerned, most cooking will be done in harbour, or at any rate at anchor, and the cook doesn't want to be stuck up forward on, say, a warm summer evening when everyone else is outside in the cockpit, either watching what is going on around them or else rejoicing in the fact that nothing is going on at all. Such isolation will only induce feelings of inferiority and persecution, with deleterious effects upon the cooking and, subsequently, everyone's digestion and temper.

In any case the yacht's lavatory will almost certainly be up forward, and it is axiomatic that the galley should be as far away from that as is reasonably possible.

Bunks

We have already said, but it will bear repeating, that there should be a full-length bunk for everyone aboard (or at least for every full-length person aboard).

Normally there will be two bunks in the cabin, and these will be used to sit on as well (such bunks are sometimes called settee berths). In the smallest cruising yachts these two bunks will probably be the total sleeping accommodation. In larger yachts there may be additional berths forward and/or aft of these. There may be one or more berths forward of the cabin. In yachts of up to five tons it is unlikely that these will be built-in or permanent berths. Instead they will probably be 'pipe cots', or a variant thereof.

A pipe cot is a sort of rigid hammock. It consists of a rectangle of piping with a piece of canvas or similar material stretched on it to form a basis for bedding. The outboard side of the rectangle is attached to the hull by some form of hinge, and when the pipe cot is ready for use the inboard side will be suspended by some means such as a long hook or a length of chain or rope. When not in use the pipe cot can be folded back against the side of the yacht, in which position it will take up a minimum of room. This is a great advantage in the narrowing space in the forward part of the yacht and is the chief reason why this kind of bunk is used there.

If there are bunks aft of the cabin these will probably be of the kind known as quarter berths (there is unlikely to be more than one of these in yachts of up to five tons). The head of such a bunk will be under the doghouse or after end of the cabin, and it will stretch aft, probably alongside the engine. Such a berth is called a quarter berth because it is located on the yacht's quarter, i.e. on her port or starboard side aft. Getting into a quarter berth can be tricky—it usually means wriggling in feet first, but they are often surprisingly roomy and comfortable, and have the additional advantage that, however violent the yacht's motion may be, it is impossible to fall out. For that matter a pipe cot, for all its crudity, can be very comfortable too, and it often happens

that the occupants of the cabin berths will not sleep as soft
as the rest of the 'crew'.

In a yacht which has a centre cockpit the arrangement of
berths will necessarily be different, and there will almost certainly be sleeping accommodation in a separate cabin aft.
But there aren't a great number of such yachts around, and
we can't afford to say any more about this aspect of them.

The number of berths in yachts of a given size will vary
a bit, but generally speaking we can expect to find two
berths in the smallest cruising yachts, and four in a five-
tonner of really modern design. The actual number will depend to a large extent on the ingenuity and intentions of the
designer, and also, as we have seen earlier on, to some extent
on the age of the yacht in question.

The subject of bunks now brings us to bedding. To start
with, cabin and quarter berths will probably have mattresses
(disguised as cushions) but the pipe cot probably won't run
to such a luxury. With regard to what you get into or pull
over yourself, this is a matter of choice—though expense
may enter into it too. You can sleep in blankets, plus a sheet
if you want to stay civilised, or you may prefer a sleeping
bag. Personally I would rather have a sleeping bag any day.
It isn't easy to dispose blankets on a bunk so that they will
stay on, and they can make a yacht very untidy below. They
are also a nuisance to fold, particularly if the weather is bad
and you can't do it outside.

I am personally of the opinion that one should sleep as
soft as possible on board, and have always had a pillow—
this can serve as a loose cushion during the day. I also always,
or at least whenever it is practicable, change into pyjamas,
simply because I think one sleeps better if one 'goes to bed'
in the normal way.

Toilet

There has been a quiet little revolution in recent years in the
'usual office' department, as in so many other aspects of
yachting. Not so long ago a large number of the yachts in

our size-range had to make do with 'galvanised sanitation'—
i.e. a bucket. I had to, on my first cruising boat, and I hasten
to add that this didn't worry me very much, but at the same
time there can be no doubt that a flush toilet is greatly to be
preferred, and these are now found on very small boats
indeed.

The one disadvantage of a flush toilet aboard a yacht is
that it has to be a fixture, and, though it may be a miniature
miracle of plumbing, it will still take up quite a lot of room.
It must also be so positioned that it can be shut off from the
rest of the yacht below decks. In yachts of five tons and less
it is not practicable to install this item in an enclosed compartment of its own. Indeed, this is often not done, or at any
rate is not done successfully, in considerably larger yachts.
I still have memories of a ten-tonner whose toilet was indeed
enclosed, but in a space so small that when the door was shut
it was impossible, for me at any rate, to sit down, which
rather destroyed the object of the exercise.

I think it is true to say that the toilet is always found in the
fore-part of a small yacht—I, at least, have never seen or
heard of one that was located anywhere else. Its normal position in our sort of yacht is in what may be loosely called the
fore-peak—i.e. the bows. The fore-peak then becomes the
W.C. compartment for the time that the meeting is in session,
so to speak, and it only remains that this compartment shall
be cut off from the cabin by some means or other(one has to
be fairly extrovert to enjoy cruising with others aboard at all,
but there are limits, and it will not always be convenient
for everyone else to go tactfully on deck). In some yachts
there will be a door between the cabin and the fore-peak,
which, of course, solves the problem. In those lacking such a
door, a curtain will probably be the answer.

Stowage
There is almost always a surprising amount of stowage space
aboard even the smallest cruising yacht, and as long as you
observe the simple rule of having a place for everything and

meticulously keeping it there when it is not in use, things should work out fairly well. It is hardly necessary to add that everything should be stowed as conveniently to hand as possible.

As a rough guide to stowage positions, sails are normally kept in the fore-peak (in easily identified bags, if possible, remember). The fore-peak will also be the natural stowage place for at least one of your warps (ropes used for mooring, etc.), for the spare anchor, if one is carried, and, of course, for the anchor chain.

Clothing will naturally be kept in the cabin, or close by— there may be, in the larger craft, suitable stowage space outside the cabin proper, perhaps between the cabin and the fore-peak. The only real problem which may arise here is the stowage of oilskins, particularly when they are wet, and a locker in which they can be hung up (commonly called a hanging locker) is a great boon. There will, however, scarcely be room for this aboard the smallest craft.

We have already mentioned the stowage of food, and seen that this will normally be somewhere at the after end of the cabin. Somewhere in the same part of the yacht, where they will keep dry but at the same time be reasonably accessible from the cockpit, you will need to keep your portable navigational instruments and related apparatus. Your steering compass will be a fixture, positioned somewhere out in the cockpit, but you may also have a hand-bearing compass, binoculars, as well as charts and their associated equipment, including navigational books and/or tables. Of these items the charts and books are the most perishable, and the satisfactory stowage of charts is not always easy in a small yacht. We will leave it at that for the time being, since we shall be having more to say on this subject in the next chapter.

There may be quite a lot of stowage space aft, in lockers around the cockpit, but this will be more or less vulnerable to the weather and should therefore be used only for those items which won't suffer too much if they get wet. The contents of these lockers may include a warp or warps (you should have at least one warp forward and one aft); tools, both for the engine and for general maintenance; buckets and scrubbers; 'smelly' items, which need to be kept outside, such as your paraffin, if you have a paraffin stove (and meths if you use this to start your stove); and, of course, your outboard, if you have a locker which will take it. Part of this space, probably that right aft, will be taken up by the fuel tank of your auxiliary engine; and if you have a gas stove the cylinder will probably be located somewhere outside too.

At the risk of being a bore I must emphasise that it is important to be as comfortable and well fed as possible on board, because tiredness and strain will sap both your physical performance and your judgement, which may lead you into making a wrong decision or into failing to do something properly. This may do no more than fray your temper—and that of your companions—but at the worst it could lead you into actual hazard. Secondly, your yacht should be as 'well-found'—i.e. well equipped—as you can make her, and you should be able to lay your hands on anything aboard— or at least on any of the more important items—without having to search for it. Playing 'hunt the saucepan' may not do more than delay your meal, but if you can't find your binoculars when you want to identify a buoy in a rough sea you could perhaps run your ship aground and place her and all aboard her in danger.

6

An Introduction to Navigation

NAVIGATION is the technique of knowing where you are, where you are going, and—all other things being equal—getting there as quickly and easily as possible.

It must be emphasised straight away that this chapter is only an introduction to the subject, even an elementary exposition of which would require much more space than we can spare in a book of this kind. What we can do, however, is, firstly, look at one or two of the basic 'tools of the trade', and, secondly, get some idea of how to use them.

The most important of all navigational aids are (a) a chart (or charts); (b) a compass.

Let us presume that, as a newcomer to cruising, you have no intention of going out of sight of land, or at any rate of some navigational mark, or not for long. Trouble can still arise on the shortest and easiest trip—even on that well-buoyed stretch of coast you have sailed up and down so many times that you know it as well as the road you live in at home.

What sort of trouble can arise? Well, to take just one example, supposing visibility is suddenly and drastically reduced by fog—which can happen on even the brightest day.

All at once you can't see the coast, or anything else.

You know where you are, of course—or you did when

the fog came down. You may decide to anchor, which may be
the best thing to do if you are safely out of the way of other
traffic and the holding ground is suitable. But you may have
to press on, if only to get out of a traffic lane.

What happens, supposing you do press on?

You can't see the land, and after a while you are not at
all sure where it is—it is so easy to lose your sense of direction
in fog at sea.

Then you have a bit of luck and come across a buoy.

You know the buoy—you know all of them in that area.
You know where the buoy is, so you know where you are
again.

But though you know the next buoy too, you can't see it,
and you don't know how it bears—i.e. in which direction it
lies—from the one you've just come across. And if you did,
you couldn't lay a course for it.

In other words, though you know where you are, you don't
know which way to go.

You sail on, and your one lonely seamark is swallowed up
in the murk astern. The buoy you hope will appear ahead
doesn't.

So now you don't know where you are *or* where you are
going, and in such circumstances all sorts of unpleasant
things can happen, from being late getting back to harbour
to not getting back at all.

The popular adage has it that it is better to travel hope-
fully than to arrive. But hope isn't much of a navigator.
You'd be much better off with a compass.

And a chart.

Let us now take a quick look at these two 'basic' aids—
and one or two ancillary ones as well.

CHARTS

A chart is a map of a sea area. If the area is a coastal one,
the coastline and some details of the land behind it will be
given. (Islands, etc., will, of course, be shown too.)

As in the case of land maps, charts are drawn to scale, the only difference in this respect being that on a chart a mile is a sea-mile (or nautical mile) of 2,000 yards, not the shorter land mile.

Again, as in the case of land maps, charts come in various scales. The larger the scale, the greater the detail. Coastal cruising in small craft normally requires the recognition of comparatively small details, so the charts commonly used by the small boat sailor will be relatively large-scale.

Longitude is marked along the top and bottom of a chart, and latitude at the sides. The latitude markings can be used as a scale for measuring distances, since on all charts 1' (one minute) of latitude equals one nautical mile. Distances should be taken from or referred to the latitude scale by using dividers (one of the necessary adjuncts of practical chart work). *The longitude scale must never be used for this purpose*, and need not concern the readers of this book.

You should have at least one chart of your sailing area. This can be either an Admiralty chart or a special yachtsmen's chart.

The Hydrographic Department of the Admiralty publishes a tremendous range of charts, covering virtually all the seas of the world—including your particular cruising ground. These charts can be obtained from Admiralty chart agents, who are to be found in all the major parts of Britain —including, of course, London.

Admiralty charts are peerless productions, comparable in authority and accuracy with our Ordnance Survey maps of the land. The appropriate Admiralty charts are perfectly adequate for yacht navigation, and in fact many yachtsmen prefer them to any others.

At the same time, Admiralty charts are, with a few small exceptions, produced primarily for the use of ships rather than yachts, whereas certain commercial firms publish charts specially for yachtsmen. (The exceptions are the Admiralty's recently published small, coloured charts of certain popular yachting harbours.)

These special yachtsmen's charts are, generally speaking, less detailed than the equivalent-scale Admiralty charts of the same areas, but they provide more information which is of specific interest to yachtsmen—yacht anchorages, for example. And they present some of their information more plainly.

For example, most of these charts are coloured, while Admiralty charts, with the exceptions mentioned above, are not. On the yachtsmen's chart the sea is coloured blue (shal-

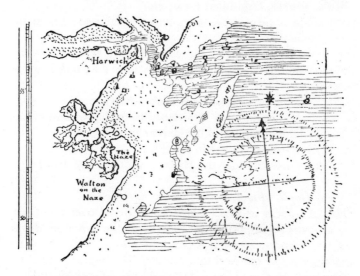

low water a light blue, and deep water a deeper blue) and drying sandbanks, etc., are shown in yellow. These colourings can be a considerable help, particularly in a shoal area (the Thames Estuary, for instance), where the many exposed sandbanks can be seen at a glance.

These special yachtsmen's charts can be obtained from the Admiralty chart agents, or from most yacht chandlers, or from their publishers.

Whether it is an Admiralty publication or not, a chart of a suitable scale will provide the yachtsman with a great deal of information about his cruising ground. This information will include details of

1. The depth of water at any given spot, plus an indication of the nature of the sea-bed at that spot.

2. Seamarks, i.e. buoys, lightships, lighthouses, etc., by which to steer or check a position.

3. Salient landmarks, which may be used for the same purpose.

4. Natural and artificial hazards, such as rocks, sandbanks, wrecks, prohibited areas, etc.

5. The nature of the tides and the tidal streams in the area.

6. Representations of the compass card (known as compass 'roses') by reference to which a course may be laid off or checked.

It may also provide such additional data as :

7. Larger-scale inset 'chartlets' illustrating or amplifying certain areas or aspects of the larger chart;

8. Recognised courses in the area.

Let us now consider the above in a little more detail :

(1) *Depth of water*

Depths appear as small numerals scattered over the chart. It is obviously important for us to know the *minimum depth* of water at any spot—it is how little, not how much, water we have under our keel that matters. The depths printed on the chart are therefore minimum depths—i.e. at low tide.

But tides vary. Some rise higher, and some fall lower, than others. To establish a standard of reference, the depths on the chart are calculated from *chart datum*, which is a low-tide level calculated from a series of tidal observations made in the area concerned, and is a level so low that only rarely and in exceptional conditions will a tide fall below it. We may accept, therefore, that the depths given on the chart represent the *normal minimum depths* in the area.

Depths may be shown in (a) fathoms—e.g. 7; sometimes plus half-fathoms—e.g. $8\frac{1}{2}$; (b) in fathoms plus feet, in which case the feet will appear as a smaller-type numeral appended to the fathom figure—e.g. 3_2, which indicates a depth of 3 fathoms plus two feet; (c) in feet. The key on the chart will state whether the depths are shown in fathoms or feet. (A fathom is, of course, six feet.)

On most charts there will be contour-lines, similar to those found on land maps, except that these will be depth-contours. These serve to give a general picture of the 'relief' of the sea-bed, and are particularly useful on charts on which differences of colour do not do this for us.

The nature or 'quality' of the sea-bed at any given spot is indicated by special standardised abbreviations, which will be explained in the key on the chart. To give a few examples, 'Cy' stands for 'clay', 'M' for mud, and 'Sn' for shingle. This information is useful as regards the holding qualities of the bottom for anchoring.

(2) *Seamarks*

These, as we already know, are points of reference within the sea area—buoys, lightships, etc.—which may be used for 'navigational'[1] purposes.

Each mark will be represented on the chart by an appropriate symbol, accompanied by an abbreviated description of the nature of the mark.

All but the most minor of these marks are differentiated, in various ways, so that each and every one can be separately identified.

Buoys: These are, generally speaking, the seamarks most frequently encountered by the yachtsman, and the ones most useful to him. They are differentiated by shape and colour, and sometimes by the further addition of lights, symbols, numbers, etc.

---

1. The word 'navigation' and its derivations are often used loosely in this book, for the sake of simplicity. The conning of a vessel in restricted or inshore waters may be more properly called 'pilotage'.

The buoys the apprentice yachtsman will come across the most frequently will be channel buoys. These, as their name indicates, are used to mark one or both sides of a navigable channel or area. They are differentiated in shape and colour according to which hand you should *leave* them on (*not* which side you should *pass* them on). The buoys which mark the starboard side of a channel, and which should be left to starboard, are called starboard-hand buoys; the buoys which mark the port side of a channel, and which should be left to port, are called port-hand buoys.

The above obviously depends on which way you are going, and the buoyage system for navigable channels is therefore based on the assumption that the above shall obtain when a vessel is entering a harbour, estuary, river, etc., from sea-ward, or, if she is proceeding coastwise, is moving in the direction of the main flood-stream. If the vessel is proceeding in the opposite direction (leaving a harbour, river, etc., or proceeding in a direction opposite to that of the main flood-stream[1]) the system will naturally be reversed.

If you are entering a harbour, river, etc., or proceeding in the direction of the main flood-stream, the channel buoys on your right or *starboard hand* will be conical in *shape*; in colour they will be *black*, or chequered black-and-white.

Certain of them may have *topmarks*, in the form of a cone or diamond on a short staff.

If they are lit, the light you see at night will be white, showing a regular series of either 1 or 3 flashes.

They may also be numbered, 1, 3, 5, etc., the numbering starting from seaward (the *port-hand* buoys on the other side of the channel will carry the alternate even numbers).

The basic distinguishing colour of *starboard-hand* buoys is *black*.

The buoys on the left or *port-hand* side of the channel, as you enter harbour or proceed in the direction of the main

1. The main flood-stream, very briefly, comes in from the Atlantic and divides to run both ways round Britain, to meet some-where in the Thames Estuary area.

flood-stream, will be *can-shaped*; in *colour* they will be *red*, or chequered red-and-white.

The topmark, if the buoy has one, will be either a small red can or a red T-shaped symbol.

The light, if any, will be either red, showing 1, 2, 3, or 4 red flashes, or white, showing 2 or 4 flashes.

They may also be numbered 2, 4, 6, etc., starting from seaward and alternating with the number of the starboard-hand buoys.

The basic distinguishing colour of *port-hand* buoys is *red*.

There are many other kinds of buoys—so many that to enumerate them all is outside the scope of this short book. Some of the most common are:

Middle ground buoys: These mark shoals which have a channel on either side.

Mid-channel buoys: These mark the centre or deepest part of a channel which is also buoyed on either side.

Wreck buoys: These mark wrecks, and are usually painted green (if a wreck buoy is lit, the light will be green).

Isolated danger buoys: These mark rocks or other hazards occurring in areas otherwise free from such perils.

The basis of the whole buoyage system is that as many of these seamarks as is practicable or necessary shall have characteristics which make them identifiable both by day and by night.

By day, buoys can be identified by their shape, colour, and perhaps a topmark; many of them also have names, which are painted on them and given on the chart.

By night, buoys can be identified by the colour of the light, and 'the way it shines'. As regards the latter, the light may be:

Fixed, in which case it will shine steadily all the time. Or it may be visible a given number of times during a definite period of time, in which case it will be either :

Flashing: Such a light will flash a given number of times during a given period; and if the flashes come in groups, it will be a *Group-flashing light.*

Occulting: Such a light will 'go out' a fixed number of times during a given period of time. If the periods of darkness when it goes out occur in groups, it will be a *Group-occulting* light.

The essential difference between a flashing and an occulting light is that the flashing light is 'out' most of the time and comes on only in brief flashes, while the occulting light is 'on' most of the time, and goes out for brief periods.

Looking down on
a sport that is
looking up – a
crow's nest view
of some of the
small craft at the
1966 Daily
Express Boat
Show

*(By courtesy of the
'Daily Express')*

TWO ENGINES
SUITABLE FOR
SMALL CRUISING
YACHTS:

i 4 B.H.P. Stuart Type P5M

(Reproduced by permission of Stuart Turner Ltd.)

ii 8 B.H.P. Stuart Type P55ME

Civilised sanitation – a Blake marine toilet suitable for small yachts

(Reproduced by permission of Blake & Sons Ltd.)

The nature or 'characteristic' of the light will be printed on the chart close to the small symbol indicating the buoy in question. For example, *R. 10 Sec*, means that this buoy or seamark shows a red flash once every ten seconds, while *Gp. Fl (3) ev. 10 secs* indicates a light which shows a group of three white flashes every ten seconds.

If the colour of the light is not stated, it will be white. If the number of flashes is not stated, the buoy will show one flash in the 'period' stated.

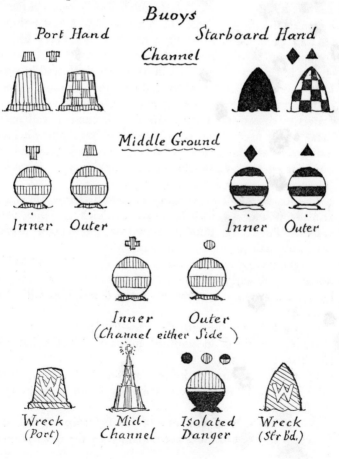

Buoys

Port Hand   Starboard Hand

Channel

Middle Ground

Inner   Outer   Inner   Outer

Inner   Outer
(Channel either Side)

Wreck   Mid-   Isolated   Wreck
(Port)   Channel   Danger   (Str'b'd.)

Certain buoys, in addition to their other characteristics are equipped with some kind of sound signal, usually a bell. The existence and nature of this signal will be noted on the chart as part of the description of the buoy in question.

The symbol on the chart and its accompanying legend will tell you everything you need to know about that particular buoy. To take an example at random from a chart I have in front of me as I write, here is a little conical symbol, with a blob on top indicating a light, and the description : *B.Gunfleet Spit Fl. ev. 15 sec. Bell.* In other words, this is a black starboard-hand buoy with the name *Gunfleet Spit* painted on it. It exhibits a white light flashing once every fifteen seconds, and it is equipped with a bell.

It is important to add that in minor channels and in very local waters—i.e. in areas which do not merit 'proper' buoys —the standard buoyage system may not be observed. In such waters starboard-hand buoys are usually conical, and port-hand buoys are usually can-shaped, but you must be prepared for variations. Some channels will not be marked by buoys at all, but by branches of trees sticking up at intervals (these are known as withies).

In such waters it is necessary to have a large-scale chart and as much local knowledge as you can pick up—plus, per-haps, a 'Pilot'. (A 'Pilot' is a marine 'guide-book' about which we shall be having more to say later.)

Larger navigational marks, such as lightships and light-houses, are described on the chart in much the same way as buoys, except that in these cases the description will also include :

(a) the height of the light above sea-level;

(b) the distance, in nautical miles, which the light is visible in clear weather;

(c) the nature and period of the sound signal employed (all such major marks give warning by sound as well as by light).

As an example of this, one of the lightship symbols on the chart in front of me is accompanied by the description :

Cork Fl. ev. 30 sec. 32 ft. 10 m. Reed ev. 20 secs. This is the Cork Lightship (her name will be painted on her in large letters) which exhibits a white flash every thirty seconds, thirty-two feet above sea-level, and visible in clear weather for ten miles; she is also equipped with a reed foghorn which in thick weather will sound once every twenty seconds.

The distance such a light is presumed to be visible in clear weather is based on calculations involving the respective heights of the light and the observer above sea-level. This need not concern the coastal cruising yachtsman. What he *should* bear in mind, however, is that lightships are sometimes withdrawn without notice.

(3) *Salient landmarks*

There is little we need say about these, except that a coastal chart will give any prominent features of the land, natural or otherwise, which may be of assistance to navigation. If such a feature is particularly prominent (a church spire, for example) it will be described on the chart as *conspic* (conspicuous).

(4) *Hazards, prohibited areas, etc.*

All hazards to navigation are (or should be) buoyed, or otherwise indicated. Prohibited areas—such as gunnery and bombing ranges—will be marked on the chart by a pecked (broken) line. In certain areas—for example, where there are submarine telephone cables—anchoring will be prohibited. This will appear on the chart in words, or abbreviated to *Anch Prohib.*

(5) *Tides and tidal streams*

To a lot of people who never get nearer the sea than a deck-chair on the beach the tide is something which comes in and goes out again (on some days it comes in and goes out further than on others and each day high water is later than the day before). If they venture to go in for a swim they may find that it is also something which carries them sideways. This

sideways movement is more likely to be that of the tidal
stream (we have already mentioned tidal streams in connection with the buoyage system).

These in-and-out and sideways movements of the sea
are intimately connected, and both are important factors
in navigation, especially in coastal waters, and therefore in
the sort of navigation most yachtsmen will be concerned
with.

The in-and-out movement of the tide means a variation in
depths of water in the area, and if the yachtsman does not
know the depths of water in the area in which he is sailing,
at the time when he is sailing there, he may find himself stuck
on a sandbank, or worse. And if he doesn't know, or doesn't
take any heed of, the sideways movement of the sea—i.e.
the direction in which the tidal stream is flowing—he may
find himself battling against it and either (a) failing
to make any headway against it at all, or (b) failing to
reach a desired point at a desired time—e.g. to catch a flood-
tide into a river or harbour; or (c) at the best, making
harder and slower work of a passage than he need have
done.

It is remarkable how many yachtsmen say, 'We'll leave
tomorrow morning at eight o'clock', without any consideration of what the tides or tidal streams will be doing at that
time and during his proposed passage. One of the disciplines
of sailing is to advance or postpone a departure in accordance with the dictates of the tides. One of the satisfactions
is to make the tides and tidal streams do as much as possible
of your work for you.

Now let us look at tides and tidal streams a little more
closely :

Tides

Most people know that the tide comes in and goes out again
twice every twenty-four hours. Like a lot of popular knowledge, this is not absolutely correct. To be more precise,
there are two high and two low waters (at most places around

the coasts of Britain) every *lunar* day, the length of which is roughly twenty-four hours fifty minutes. (This is why high water is later each day than the day before.)

There are different tides at some places around our own coasts, but these need not concern us here.

Range

The *vertical difference* between one high tide (generally known as high water) and the next low tide (low water) is called the range of the tide.

The range of the tide varies according to the influence of heavenly bodies upon the sea—and, therefore, according to the day of the lunar month. And for any given date it will vary from place to place—the tides have a greater range in the Channel Islands, for example, than they do on the east coast of England.

Movements of the sea are influenced by the moon, and to a lesser degree the sun. When these two heavenly bodies are in line, or nearly in line, which happens at new and full moon every lunar month—i.e. twice every such month—they exercise their greatest influence, and shortly after these dates (about a day and a half after), because the influence of these heavenly bodies upon the sea is a delayed one, we get a peak tide.

Such a tide is called a *spring tide*. Spring tides have nothing to do with the season of the year, but occur regularly twice every lunar month.

From the 'optimum' positions in which they create a spring tide, the sun and moon then move more and more out of line, their influence upon the sea becomes correspondingly less, and the tides will rise and fall less and less, until a time is reached when, shortly after the sun and moon have reached positions at which they are at right-angles to each other, and their influence is at a minimum, the range of the tide will fall to its minimum.

Such tides are known as *neap tides*, and they occur, like spring tides, twice every lunar month.

Then, after a neap tide, the range of the tide will increase again until the next spring tide is reached. And so on.

An elementary but important fact to remember is that the higher the tide rises, the lower it will fall, and that at low water on a spring tide, therefore, there will—other circumstances being normal—be a less depth of water at any one spot than there will be at any other time during the tide cycle.

The yachtsman's concern is to know what depth of water there will be at any particular spot at any particular time. The chart will tell him the *minimum* depth in the area, and he can calculate the depth there will be there at any given time by using tide-tables.

Tide-tables

Briefly, a tide-table is a calendar giving the daily heights and times of high and low water at a 'standard' port, or ports (Dover is such a port), with additional tables by means of which the heights and times of the tide in subsidiary areas can be calculated.

If you are cruising locally you should be able to make do with the simple tide-tables published for your area. These are usually obtainable from yacht chandlers or boat yards.

Such a tide-table will give the times and heights of the tides at the nearest 'standard' port, together with time-and-height differences for various places within your own area, and the calculating procedure for finding the depth of water, at any particular spot in your area at any particular time, is very simple.

Later, when you are going further afield, you may need to use tide-tables published by the Admiralty.

A good deal of useful information about tides may be given on your chart. To refer again to the one I have on my desk at the moment, this tabulates the range of the tide at 'springs' and 'neaps', at twenty-five places in the area covered by the chart, together with the time-difference at each compared with the most convenient 'standard port', which in this case is Dover. To find the time and height of high water at any of these places for any particular tide it is therefore only necessary to look up the time of high water at Dover and apply the differences noted on the chart. The height of the tide plus the depth printed on the chart will give you depth of water in any given spot.

Taking this a stage further, you can estimate how much water there will be in any given area at any specified time between high and low water. The word 'estimate' is used here rather than 'calculate', because the last stage of this operation is not a very precise one. There are ways of calculating how much a tide will rise or fall in a given time, but the results are not always accurate, particularly in coastal waters, where other influences may affect the situation considerably.

All the yachtsman need remember is that the rate of rise or fall of a tide varies, that it will start and end slowly, and that the rate of rise or fall will be greatest at about half-tide. Converted into practical terms, this means that he can expect the tide to have risen or fallen by about half its range by half-flood or half-ebb; that depths will be slow to take off from high water and, more to the point, equally slow to increase from low water; also that trying to skate over a shallow patch at half-ebb or thereabouts will be asking for trouble! (The golden rule here is that if you *must* cross a dubious shoal area you should do so only on a rising tide.)

Tidal streams

The influences of the sun and the moon which cause tides are also responsible for the tidal streams.

On an indented coast, and particularly in an area where there are rivers, estuaries, etc.—in other words, in the sort of areas which are favoured by the majority of cruising yachtsmen—the tidal streams are largely identifiable with the tide in the area, i.e. they will 'flood' into the river or estuary and 'ebb' out again.

Like tides, tidal streams run for a certain period in each

direction, and their rate of movement varies during their
period. Tables exist from which these rates can be ascertained
and information about them may also appear on the chart—
again with reference to the time of high water at a standard
port. You can therefore work out the strength and direction
of the tidal stream in any specified area at any specified
time.

The chart symbol for a tidal stream is an arrow pointing
in the direction in which the stream is running at a particular
time, at springs and neaps, with the rate in knots printed
along it. On some charts information about the tidal streams
in the area will be given in a series of inset chartlets for each
hour of the run of the flood and the ebb—e.g. *five hours
before H.W. (High Water) at Dover. . . . four hours before
H.W. at Dover . . . one hour after H.W. at Dover . . . two
hours after H.W. at Dover,* etc., etc.

Tidal streams may not matter a great deal to ships or
high-powered motor-yachts, etc., but, as has been indicated
earlier, they are important to small vessels under sail.

A very simple example will illustrate this. Suppose you
have a breeze which is pushing your yacht along at five
knots. This will be your *speed through the water.* But it is
your *speed over the ground*—i.e. over the sea-bed—which
counts as regards the distance you make good. If you have
a two-knot stream wholly with you, your speed over the
ground will be $5 + 2$ knots $= 7$ knots, while if the stream
is dead against you, you will only make good $5 - 2$ knots
$= 3$ knots. In other words, in these circumstances you will
be covering the distance more than twice as fast if you have
the stream with you.

One of the great arts and satisfactions of sailing is always
to try to get the wind and the sea as much on your side as
possible. They will still manage to oppose you quite often
enough!

Compass roses
Every chart—except some large-scale harbour plans, etc.—

will have several representations of the compass card printed on it. These are called compass 'roses', and they are there to refer to for navigational purposes (the way they are used will be described in the next chapter).

These roses will be so disposed that convenient reference can be made to one or other of them from any point on the chart. On coastal charts one or more of these roses may be printed on that part of the chart which represents land. Their position has no other significance than that they shall be convenient for practical reference.

Inset chartlets

These have already been referred to, and they are virtually self-explanatory. Such insets on a larger chart may be used to delineate a particular area in greater detail, or they may be used to convey specific information—e.g. as in the case of tidal streams.

Recognised courses

The delineation of courses on a chart is a convenience in that some of your navigation may thus be done for you. Such a course will be shown by a straight line. Alongside the course-line there may appear information such as the names of the marks the course runs between, with the distance between them and the compass course to steer.

You may, if you have a chart which gives such courses, do a very elementary practical exercise—a baptism in practical chart work, so to speak. With a pair of dividers (which one uses in chart work for measuring distance), check the distance or distances given alongside a course or courses on the chart against the latitude scale at one side or other of the chart, remembering that 1′ on the latitude scale equals one nautical mile.

Chart correction

Charts, like maps of the land, will inevitably become inaccurate with the passing of time. For example, a sandbank in an estuary or off the coast may shift, necessitating the moving of buoys or a light-vessel or other navigational marks. Artificial hazards such as wrecks and constructions of various kinds may make their appearance.

If you use an inaccurate land map you will at the worst only get lost, but an inaccurate chart may lead you into danger. It is essential, therefore, that the chart or charts you are using should be up to date.

This does not mean that you must keep on buying new charts. The accepted practice is to correct the charts you have—if they are not too old or so strewn with corrections already as to make them difficult to use.

The standard practice for correcting a chart is to pick out the relevant corrections from the Admiralty's *Notices To Mariners* and transfer them to the chart.

These *Notices To Mariners* are a series of pamphlets published weekly, giving details of the latest navigational changes. The pamphlets cover all the changes affecting all the charts the Admiralty publishes, including any important ones in your own area.

The *Notices* can be obtained from Admiralty chart agents and certain other offices in most of Britain's ports, but it is scarcely necessary for the cruising yachtsman to wade through all of them. It should be possible for him to obtain information about those changes which affect him from a local source. Many yacht clubs keep available to their members those *Notices* which affect their area.

On every chart there is printed the date to which it was corrected before publication—it will carry a line something like: *This chart has been corrected up to 1.6.65 and should be used in conjunction with Admiralty Notices To Mariners.* In other words, it is up to you to find out what changes, if any, there have been in that area since that date, and to correct the chart accordingly. If you don't want the trouble of doing this yourself, you can have it done for you by a chart agent, for a not unreasonable fee.

So—keep your charts as up-to-date as possible. And remember that, though nothing may be happening 'yachting-wise' during winter, when your boat is laid up, a great deal may be happening at sea. Changes in the configuration of the sea-bed and the additions of new hazards such as wrecks are most likely to occur during the heavy weather of winter, and a number of corrections to your charts may consequently be necessary before the start of a new season. If you take care to see that your charts are corrected to date at the beginning of the new season you will have only an occasional correction, if any, to make during the month you are afloat.

Two last thoughts about charts:
(1) *Master chart*
The signs and symbols used on Admiralty charts in general are given on Admiralty chart No. 5011. This is a 'master-chart' in this respect, and provides a wealth of information.

(2) *Chart table: stowage of charts*
When you get to the stage of doing practical navigation you will need a 'chart table' to work on.

Finding room for a chart table—even if it is no more than a flat board—is a problem in a small yacht, but you should try to accommodate one of dimensions not less than about 2 ft. × 2 ft. 6 in. It is important that charts be kept as flat as possible, and without too many folds.

The chart table should be below decks, preferably near the cockpit, for ease of communication with or access to and from the steering position. It should be positioned length-wise, i.e. when it is in use, the fore-and-aft dimension should be the longer one.

The table can be either portable or hinged to the side of the yacht. In my five-tonner it was hinged to the side and could be folded down flat over the starboard quarter berth, which was a satisfactory position in that the navigator was about as close to the cockpit as he could be, and, with the doghouse over him, had room to work.

The disadvantage of this arrangement was that it pro-

vided no chart stowage, which is an important consideration. If the chart table has to be portable its stowage may
be a problem in itself, but in this case a virtue may be made
of necessity by having the table made in the form of a very
shallow box—it need not be more than one inch deep—
inside which the charts themselves can be stowed.

Some of the special yachtmen's charts are made to fold
up quite small, rather like a motoring map, but these are not
very suitable for practical work. Nor, for that matter, is a
coloured chart as suitable as a black-and-white one, for the
simple reason that the navigational work on it, which should
be done with a comparatively soft pencil, will not show up
so well.

Charts should not be stowed rolled up if this can possibly
be avoided.

Chart work—equipment

For practical work on the chart you will require, in addition
to a chart table to work on, the following equipment:

(a) A parallel ruler: the way to use this will be explained
later.

(b) Pencils and rubber: the pencils should not be too
hard, since the work on the chart will be rubbed out again
after it has served its purpose so that the chart will be clean
for further work in the same area at a later date. For the
same reason you should work as lightly as is consistent with
clarity and accuracy.

(c) Dividers: these, as we have seen already, are used
for measuring distances.

So much for the first of our two basic 'aids' to navigation.
This may be a suitable place, however, to mention two other
important and complementary sources of information:

(1) *'Pilots'*

The Admiralty produces a series of publications known as
'Pilots'. These are not pamphlets, like the *Notices To
Mariners,* but stout volumes. The whole series covers the

coasts of the world—again, as in the case of charts, including your sailing ground.

Each chapter of a 'Pilot' (after a general, introductory one) gives details of a section of the coast and coastal waters covered by the particular volume. The information given includes details of the topography of the coast, of tides and tidal streams, dangers, storm signals, buoys, beacons, other navigational marks, etc., etc. It also contains 'visual' information such as harbour plans, and a series of views of the coastline from seaward which add up to a continuous picture of the whole length of coast covered by that volume.

The reader will realise that a lot of this information also appears on the charts of the area, but there is also a good deal which doesn't. The two kinds of publication are essentially complementary and should be used in conjunction.

There are also other 'Pilots' which are not published by the Admiralty. One I have found particularly useful is *The Pilot's Guide To The Thames Estuary and Norfolk Broads,* which is published by Imray, Laurie, Norie and Wilson Ltd. (The same firm also publishes a companion volume entitled *The Pilot's Guide To The English Channel.*) This kind of publication is intended specially for yachtsmen, and is therefore, as in the case of the special yachtsmen's charts—a series of which, incidentally, are published by the same firm—in some respects more suitable for the small boat sailor than the Admiralty 'Pilots' which are intended primarily for shipping.

The newcomer to cruising will be well advised to acquire, as soon as possible, the most suitable chart or charts of his area, and the appropriate 'Pilot' or 'Pilots', and study them carefully. In this way you will in time get to know your sailing ground intimately—and you can hardly know it too well. A 'Pilot' in particular can be fascinating and profitable reading for winter evenings—and if the book leads you to 'dream yourself afloat', that won't do you any harm either!

It is a wise principle to get to know as much as is reasonably possible about any area before you actually take your craft into it. If you are planning a trip you haven't done before—even if it is only a very modest extension of an earlier one, involving no real navigation—read it up beforehand. You may not have the time, or conditions may make it difficult, for you to make extensive reference to your sources of information when you are actually 'on passage'.

This may be a suitable place to mention one more type of reference book which is, or will one day be, an indispensable part of your sailing library. This is a 'nautical almanack'. These volumes contain a wealth of data on every aspect of navigation and pilotage. (The best known of them is Reed's Nautical Almanack.) A nautical almanack is apt to appear somewhat formidable to the novice, but with a little practice you will soon be able to find your way about in it.

The second of our basic aids, as we have already seen, is the compass.

Various types of compass are used aboard yachts, but they are all generally the same—i.e. they are all magnetic compasses. Each will consist essentially of a circular, graduated card floating in a bowl of liquid, the bowl being gimballed (i.e. suspended) so that it will maintain the horizontal against the roll and/or pitch of the yacht.

These compasses are called magnetic because 'North' on the compass card points to 'magnetic' North, as opposed to 'true' North. Compasses which indicate true north are elaborate and extremely expensive pieces of power-operated mechanism suitable only for ships—or yachts approximating to ships.

The difference between magnetic North and true North will be explained later.

The compass card

The card of the magnetic compass can be read in accordance with any of three different systems of notation. These are

(1) the point system; (2) the three-figure system; (3) the quadrantral system.

1. In the point system the complete circumference of the compass card (360°) is divided into 32 points, one point therefore being 11¼°. These points read North (N), North by East (N × E), North North East (NNE), North East

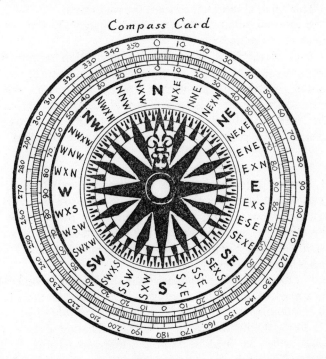

Compass Card

by North (NE × N), North East (NE), North East by East NE × E), East North East (ENE), East by North (E × N), etc. North, East, South, and West are, of course, the 'Cardinal Points'.

2. In the three-figure system the card is graduated by degrees clockwise from North (000°), and readings are taken in degrees. This is the simplest system and the most accurate, and therefore generally the most practicable.

Both the above notations will appear on the same card. In the three-figure notation the total circumference is divided into 5° sections, numbered in tens of degrees.

3. The quadrantal system uses a combination of cardinal points and degrees to describe direction, e.g. North East would be N.45°E.

This method need not concern the yachtsman.

A representation of the card of the magnetic compass is shown on page 95.

Two of the basic procedures of navigation require the use of a compass. These are (a) steering a course; (b) determining, or checking, the yacht's position. For reasons which will shortly appear, it is seldom possible to use one compass for both procedures, and two will therefore be required, namely (1) a steering compass; (2) a bearing compass.

Steering compass

A steering compass indicates the direction in which your craft is heading. For this, two components are necessary: (1) the compass card, which is your static reference as to direction; (2) an indication of the fore-and-aft line of your yacht—i.e. the direction in which she is pointing at any time; this is known as the *ship's head*.

On most magnetic compasses the ship's head is indicated by a mark of some kind—usually a line painted on the inside of the compass bowl. This is known as the *lubber-line*.

Obviously the lubber-line, being an indication of the ship's head, must be lined up with the fore-and-aft line of the yacht. Therefore the steering compass must be either (and preferably) a fixture; or, if it is portable, it must always be shipped in a predetermined, lined-up position.

In order to steer in any given direction it is only necessary to alter course until the lubber-line on the compass bowl coincides with the indication of the required direction on the graduated compass card; e.g. in order to steer North, one has only to bring the lubber-line opposite North on the compass card.

It is worth remembering that, although the compass card appears to move round when an alteration of course is made, this is only an illusion. The compass card is, as we have already said, the static component—North on the compass card always points to North. The yacht, on the other hand, may be pointing north, south, east, west, or in any inter- mediate direction. The yacht is the variable, and it is the *yacht which moves* round the compass card; or, as my old Navy instructor used to say, in his inimitable way, 'the com- pass card don't go round nothing'.

Grid compasses

One drawback of the ordinary magnetic compass in a yacht which has tiller steering—and that means the great majority of the yachts we are concerned with in this book—is that, although the position of the compass is and must be fixed, the helmsman's viewing position will vary according to his steering position in the cockpit, and he will therefore sight the compass card from various angles. This can produce a visual error (just as if one views a clock-face from one side and then the other, and if there is some clearance be- tween the minute hand and the clock-face, the observed time may appear to vary slightly).

This error, which is known as *parallax*, can be overcome by using a grid compass. Very briefly, with this type of com- pass the course to steer is pre-set by means of a rotatable grid on the top of the compass bowl; the lubber-line runs across the diameter of the compass, and in order to steer the pre-set course it is only necessary to keep the lubber-line parallel with the lines of the grid.

The parallax error is not large, however, and on short courses such as those sailed by most coastal yachtsmen the resultant error in position will not be worth bothering about. Grid compasses are only mentioned here because many of these have come on to the market as war surplus equipment, and are therefore a cheap alternative to the 'standard' com- pass.

G

For ease of viewing, a steering compass may have a small glass prism or similar attachment which magnifies the lubber-line and a small portion of the compass card on either side of it. It may have a hood, to make the card easier to see in bright sunlight. For use at night it should be suitably illumi-nated—from the bottom of the bowl, but not too brightly, to avoid eye-strain.

Compass deviation

A magnetic compass, by virtue of the very fact that it *is* magnetic, will be influenced by any iron or steel aboard the yacht, either in her construction or otherwise, and also by any equipment containing magnets.

The effect of these influences will be to deflect the needle of the compass from magnetic North, and this deflection, which is called deviation, will vary with the yacht's heading.

Deviation must be allowed for in any serious, long-distance navigation, and for this purpose a deviation table must be prepared. This is done by 'swinging the compass'—i.e. by putting the vessel on various known headings round the com-pass and noting the difference between the bearing of mag-netic North on the chart and the bearing indicated by the compass needle.

A deviation table need only be drawn up once—unless there is any significant alteration in the positions of the metal content of the vessel.

If a compass is properly positioned—i.e. if it is so placed that the secondary magnetic influences will be at a mini-mum, the error due to deviation will not be large, and again, as far as the beginner yachtsman is concerned at any rate, it may be ignored.

Bearing compass

As has already been stated, each of the two navigational procedures of (a) steering and (b) determining ('fixing') a vessel's position requires the employment of a compass.

There is no reason why bearings should not be taken with

the steering compass, except that the operation involves sighting horizontally across the compass bowl, and in small yachts the steering compass is not likely to be installed in a position which makes this possible. A separate compass is therefore necessary for taking bearings. This compass is held in the hand when in use, and is therefore known as a *hand-bearing compass*.

The normal hand-bearing compass is a small magnetic compass—usually smaller than the steering compass—with a handle attachment underneath containing an electric battery for illuminating the compass card at night. There is an engraved line on the inside of the bowl, similar to the lubber-line on the steering compass, and a notched, magnifying prism, again similar to that on the steering compass, to make it easier to read off the bearing.

To take a compass bearing of an object, the latter is sighted horizontally across the bowl of the compass, through the notch in the prism (which may be compared to a rifle sight). In the prism you will see a magnified reflected image of part of the compass card and of the engraved line on the compass bowl. With the object centred in the notch, read off where the engraved line cuts the compass card. This reading is *the bearing of the object from the yacht*.

Since a hand-bearing compass is magnetic, it will be subject to the same secondary magnetic influences as the steering compass, but, since it is portable, a position for using it can be found (by experiment) at which the sum of these influences is at a minimum. Deviation is not normally allowed for when using a hand-bearing compass.

7

Navigation—Basic Procedures

WHILE it is not practicable within the scope of this book to pursue even the elements of navigation much further, we can perhaps just look at two fundamental procedures sufficiently to enable the beginner to practise the rudiments of them and thus gain a little initial confidence in his 'instruments' (and himself).

These two procedures are (1) laying a course—i.e. working out the direction to steer; (2) 'fixing' your yacht's position—i.e. determining her position at any given time.

(1) *Laying a course*
A vessel under way may be subject to one or both of two lateral influences. These are (1) leeway, i.e. the distance she may be pushed sideways by the pressure of the wind; (2) the distance she may be carried sideways by an obliquely running tidal stream.

Both these influences may have to be allowed for when laying a course, but for the sake of simplicity we will assume here that the yacht is sailing in conditions when neither of them affect her—e.g. when she is sailing with a following wind (in which case she will make no leeway) and when she is proceeding either directly with, or dead against, the tidal stream, which will then have no lateral effect upon her.

Finding the compass course to steer involves reference to one of the compass roses on your chart of the area. This is done by using a parallel ruler.

There are various kinds of parallel ruler, but the two most common kinds are the bar type (Fig. a) and the roller type (Fig. b). The principle of paralled rules is that they can be 'walked', in the case of the bar type, or rolled (the

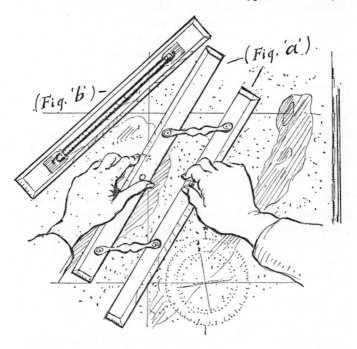

(Fig. 'a')

(Fig. 'b')

roller type), across the chart and remain parallel to their original lie on the chart.

To find the compass course to steer, the actual course is first drawn as a straight pencil line on the chart. This course-line is drawn from the yacht's present position (this must be known), with the parallel ruler, which is then carefully 'walked', or rolled, according to type, to the nearest compass rose until the nearer edge of the ruler cuts through the centre

of the rose. The magnetic course to steer can then be read
from where the same edge of the ruler cuts the circumference
of the compass rose, in the required direction.

NOTE 1. The above holds good for charts on which the
compass rose gives magnetic bearings only. On some charts
the rose will show two concentric circles. In such cases the
inner rose will give magnetic bearings and the outer one true
bearings. Since the yachtsmen has a magnetic compass, he
should use the inner circle and ignore the outer one.

The inner circle gives bearings in three-figure notation
(degrees) outside it, and in points notation inside it.

NOTE 2. We have already seen that the magnetic compass used for steering is subject to a margin of error known
as *deviation*, and that navigation requires that a correction
in the course to steer must be made for this. Reference to
the compass rose will reveal another modifying factor. This
is known as *variation*.

Variation. Magnetic North does not coincide with true
North, and the difference between the two, expressed in degrees and minutes, is known as the *variation*. There is a com-
plication here too, in that the magnetic poles which influence
the magnetic compass are not fixed in position but move
about. This means that the variation between true and
magnetic North is constantly changing.

The variation and the rate of change will be printed along
the West East axis of the compass rose—e.g. *Var*". $7°25'$
W (1957) decreasing 7.5 annually.

The basic variation here does not concern the yachtsman,
because all his observations will be magnetic, and the annual
rate of change is so small that this need be taken into consideration only for precision work.

For our present purposes, *both deviation and variation
may be ignored,* but it is important for the 'beginner' yachtsman to realise that these complications exist.

Exercise

As a very elementary exercise in finding the course to steer, choose a time when your yacht is in a known position—e.g. when you are close to a known buoy.

With a pencil and your parallel ruler, draw a straight line on the chart from your present position to an objective— perhaps a neighbouring buoy. Now 'walk' or roll your ruler to the nearest compass rose in the manner already described and read off the course to steer. Put your yacht on this compass course, and you should be heading for your objective.

You have now done your first bit of practical navigation, and your first bit of sailing 'by instruments'. It is worth noting that even this very simple procedure would give you a fair chance, if fog came down as described in Chapter 6, of finding your next navigational mark.

(2) *'Fixing' a position*

There are various ways of doing this. We will confine ourselves here to the simplest visual 'fix', which will at least serve

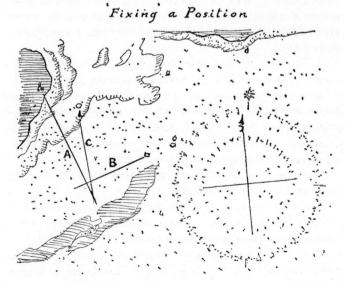

Fixing a Position

to provide an illustration of the use of the hand-bearing compass.

Such a fix is obtained by taking bearings of at least two visual objects. The operation may be broken up into the following steps :

1. Choose two visual marks as nearly as possible at right-angles to each other and identify them on the chart. Let us call these marks A and B. Perhaps A is a lighthouse and B a buoy.

2. Using the hand-bearing compass, take the bearing of the lighthouse (A).

Now lay your parallel ruler across the diameter of the compass rose on the chart nearest to A so that one edge cuts the magnetic circle of the rose on the bearing you have taken.

3. 'Walk' or roll the parallel ruler across the chart until its nearer edge cuts through A.

4. With the parallel ruler, draw a line on the chart from A towards and through your roughly estimated position.

This is known as a position line. Since this line represents your line-of-sight of the object A, your yacht must lie somewhere along it. But at what point along it you do not yet know, because you have as yet got only one component of your fix.

5. Now repeat the procedure with the second of your marks (the buoy B): i.e. take the bearing of B with the hand-bearing compass; lay the parallel ruler on the nearest compass rose to B so that it cuts the magnetic circle of the rose on the bearing taken; 'walk' or roll the parallel ruler across the chart until its nearer edge cuts through B; draw a line on the chart from B until it cuts the first.

You now have a second position line. In other words, your craft must be somewhere along this line.

It will be obvious now that the only place at which your craft can be on both these lines is where they intersect. This is your position, and you have obtained it by a visual 'fix'.

The reason for choosing two objects as nearly at right-angles as possible is to give the largest possible angle of intersection, and therefore the smallest margin of error. If the two objects are close together, the angle between them will be less sharp and the point of intersection may be correspondingly less precise.

If there is a third and convenient visual object (C) in the area, you can take the bearing of this as a check. The procedure is the same as before; namely, take the bearing of C with the hand-bearing compass and then, using the parallel ruler, draw a third position line from C to cut the other two.

It is virtually impossible to take bearings with absolute precision, so it is most unlikely that your third position line will pass through the point of intersection of the other two. Instead the position lines will intersect to form a triangle.

This triangle is known navigationally as a 'cocked hat'. If the cocked hat is small, you may assume that your fixing of your position has been done correctly and with reasonable precision, and you may take it that your yacht's position lies somewhere within the triangle. A large 'cocked hat' will indicate you have not carried out the fixing procedure with sufficient precision.

Exercise

Choose a time when your craft is in a known position and with two or three visual marks from which you can obtain position lines. Take bearings of these marks and draw the resultant position lines on the chart. If you have done things correctly and with reasonable accuracy the position lines should intersect or form a small cocked hat at or near your known position.

NOTE 1. *Transits*: When two objects or marks which are identifiable on the chart and which are not too close together appear in line to the observer, a position line may be obtained simply by drawing a straight line through the marks in question and extending it through his own estimated position. This obviates the need to use the hand-bearing compass. A second position line obtained with the aid of the hand-bearing compass will enable a fix to be obtained.

NOTE 2. Fixes may be obtained by night as well as day from navigational and sometimes other lights. The hand-bearing compass is illuminated for this purpose.

NOTE 3. Fixes may also be obtained by using D.F. radio apparatus to receive signals transmitted by marine radio beacons, but such apparatus need not concern the cruising beginner.

Other navigational equipment :

Patent log : This is a piece of equipment for measuring the distance the yacht sails *through the water*. It consists essenti-ally of a finned rotator which is towed astern on a line which is connected to a dial fixed to the yacht somewhere at the stern—usually on her transom. The pull on the rotator as the yacht moves through the water causes it to revolve, and this in turn causes the towing line to rotate and to register these revolutions on the dial in terms of distance.

This apparatus is required only when there is no other way of measuring or estimating the distance sailed with reasonable accuracy, and is necessary only for rather more extended cruising than we are concerned with in this book.

The important thing to remember about the patent log, when you come to use it, is that, as we have already em-phasised above, the distance registered is the *distance sailed through the water,* and corrections will have to be applied to find the *distance made good over the ground* (i.e. the sea-bed), which is what matters as far as the yacht's position is concerned.

Sounding equipment
Depths at sea are known as soundings, and sounding equip-ment is used to measure depth.

Soundings may be taken in one of three ways :

1. By means of a lead line (properly a 'boat's lead and line').

This consists of a line with a lead sinker attached to it, the line being marked distinctively at certain depths.

The standard markings are, from the sinker upwards :

At 1 fathom ...	1 short strip of leather (tucked through the line)
At 2 fathoms...	2 strips of leather
At 3 fathoms...	3 strips of leather .
At 5 fathoms...	A short piece of white cloth
At 7 fathoms...	A piece of red cloth
At 10 fathoms...	A piece of leather with a hole in it
At 13 fathoms...	A piece of blue cloth

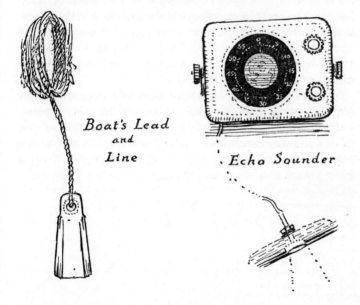

Boat's Lead and Line

Echo Sounder

The first three fathoms—where niceties of depth are important—are marked in feet by pieces of cord in each of which there are knots equal to the number of feet recorded—i.e. 1, 2, 3, 4, 5.

These markings may at first sight seem somewhat eccentric, and unnecessarily complicated, but the object is to ensure that the depth recorded shall be quickly discoverable by some indication which cannot be confused with any other.

Some yachtsmen use 'home-made' lead lines which do not conform to this pattern, but the advantage of the standard pattern is that it can be used even by a stranger aboard, so long as he is familiar with the accepted markings.

2. Soundings may be made electrically, by means of an instrument known as an *echo-sounder*. Small and relatively cheap instruments of this kind are now obtainable for installation aboard small craft.

The great advantage of an echo-sounder is that it will give a continuous, at-a-glance indication of the depth of water beneath the craft in question. Its disadvantage is that, being a piece of mechanical-electrical equipment, it may go wrong.

A boat's lead and line will not go wrong. Even if your yacht has an echo-sounder, therefore, you should always carry a lead and line as a stand-by.

3. Some yachtsmen, especially those who have a penchant for 'ditch-crawling'—i.e. sailing in very shallow waters— carry a sounding pole, which is simply a graduated pole with which the depth may be checked. This is a very simple method of sounding, but such a pole is an unhandy thing to have aboard a small cruising yacht.

8

The Rule of the Road at Sea

So far we have been concerned, from the navigational point of view, with what we may for convenience call 'static' dangers. It is now time to take a look at the other, or 'mobile', hazards.

A vital element in your handling of your yacht will be a knowledge of how to direct her course with relation to other vessels in the vicinity. *This involves knowing what you should do and what the other vessel or vessels should do in any given circumstances.*

The procedures to be followed by two (or more) vessels in proximity are governed by the 'rules of the road at sea'. This is a 'seaway code', and fulfils the same function as the Highway Code on land.

This seaway code is obtainable in its latest form at the time of writing in a pamphlet entitled *The Collision Regulations (Ships and Seaplanes on the Water) and Signals of Distress (Ships) Order 1965*, published by Her Majesty's Stationery Office. These regulations were agreed by the International Conference on Safety of Life at Sea, 1960, and came into force on September 1st, 1965.

Before we look at the regulations themselves, several points of the utmost importance must be made :

When two vessels are approaching each other, one will have precedence over the other.

The persons in control of both vessels at the time must know which has precedence.

The vessel which has precedence must 'stand on'—i.e. maintain her course and speed. This gives the other vessel a basis for her own actions.

The other vessel must 'give way'—i.e. take avoiding action.

The vessel which has to give way must alter course (or stop, or go astern) *in ample time* for the other vessel to become aware of her intention.

The one vessel must at all times know what the other is doing or is going to do.

Now let us take a brief look at the Rules themselves. It is not necessary for the yachtsman to know them all by heart —there are thirty-one of them altogether, and some of them are complicated. But he should be acquainted with them all, and have a thorough knowledge of those which are most likely to apply to him.

First of all, it is necessary for the one vessel to be able to identify the other in three basic respects. Generally speaking, power-driven vessels have to give way to sail, so firstly it is necessary to discover the means of propulsion of the other vessel. Secondly, it is necessary to know if she is a large vessel; and, thirdly, whether she is or is not capable of manœuvring freely.

By day the size of a vessel and her means of propulsion will be obvious, and if she is not capable of manœuvring freely, she will exhibit certain symbols known as 'shapes'. By night all these items of information will be conveyed by lights.

After Rule 1, therefore, which comes under the heading *Preliminary and Definitions* because it introduces and defines the 'terms of reference' of the Rules in general, there follows a group of rules (Rules 2–14) headed *Lights and Shapes*.

Lights and Shapes
Rule 2 describes the lights which power-driven vessels shall

carry when under way. A distinction is made here between vessels over and under 150 feet in length.

Rule 3 describes the light a power-driven vessel shall carry by night when towing or pushing another vessel, and the 'shape' she shall exhibit by day. (The shape in this instance is a black diamond.)

Rule 4 describes the lights and shapes which shall be exhibited by (1) a vessel not under command; (2) a vessel engaged on submarine cable operations; (3) a vessel engaged in minesweeping operations.

These three conditions are grouped together because in all three cases the vessel concerned will not be able to manœuvre easily and normally, and therefore cannot be expected to take safe avoiding action.

Rule 5 describes the lights which shall or may be carried by a sailing vessel under way, the lights she shall carry when being pushed ahead, and the shape she shall exhibit when being towed by day.

Rule 6 makes provision for exhibiting side lights (red— port and green—starboard) only temporarily in bad weather.

Rule 7 describes the lights, alternative to those already described, which may be carried by smaller vessels (under sixty-five feet in length), and the appropriate day signals for when they are not proceeding under their own power.

Rule 8 describes the lights to be carried by pilot vessels.

Rule 9 describes the lights and shapes to be carried by fishing vessels.

Rule 10 describes the stern lights which vessels shall carry.

Rule 11 describes the lights (and day signals) to be exhibited by vessels (1) at anchor; (2) engaged on submarine cable operations; (3) aground.

Rule 12 describes the lights and/or signals a vessel may employ to attract attention.

Rule 13 makes provision for special circumstances with regard to the above group of rules.

Rule 14 specifies the day symbol to be exhibited by a vessel proceeding under sail and power.

The next group of the Rules (a small group of only two, namely Rules 15 and 16) are those to be observed in fog or bad visibility :

Sound signals and conduct in restricted visibility.

Rule 16 details the manœuvring procedure for fog or bad weather.

Next follows a group of Rules (Rules 17–27) under the head of *Steering and Sailing Rules*. These rules describe the rule of the road for vessels in situations in which there is a danger of collision—i.e. when the distance between them is closing.

This group of the Rules is more important to the yachtsman than any other, and of the group *Rule 17* is the most important of all because it details the action to be taken by sailing vessels when the risk of collision exists between them. This is the collision situation most likely to be experienced by a yachtsman, since he will almost certainly find himself more often in this situation with regard to other yachts than any other craft.

This group of Rules is introduced by a number of preliminary remarks, two of which are of the greatest importance to all who have vessels under their command :

1. *In obeying and construing these Rules, any action taken should be positive, in ample time, and with due regard to the observance of good seamanship.*

2. *Risk of collision can, when circumstances permit, be ascertained by carefully watching the compass bearing of an approaching vessel. If the bearing does not appreciably change, such risk should be deemed to exist.*

NOTE : This sort of situation can be checked, initially at any rate, without using a compass. If the other vessel can be seen to be drawing forward or aft, then the two vessels are not on a collision course.

A two-and-a-half-ton two-berth
Silhouette – a popular 'baby'
cruiser

Another view of the above craft

Grid steering compass

(*By courtesy South Western Marine Factors Ltd.*)

Steering compass   Hand bearing compass

Rule 17 should be known by heart, so here it is in full :

Rule 17 (a) WHEN TWO SAILING VESSELS ARE APPROACH-
ING ONE ANOTHER SO AS TO INVOLVE RISK OF COLLISION,
ONE OF THEM SHALL KEEP OUT OF THE WAY OF THE OTHER
AS FOLLOWS :

   (i) WHEN EACH HAS THE WIND ON A DIFFERENT SIDE,
      THE VESSEL WHICH HAS THE WIND ON THE PORT
      SIDE SHALL KEEP OUT OF THE WAY OF THE OTHER.

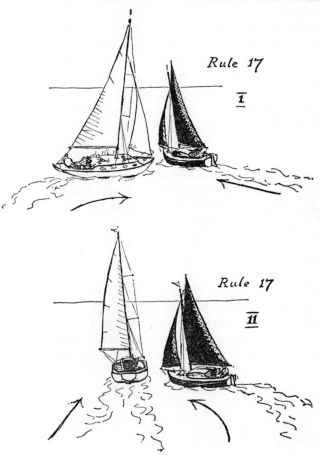

Rule 17

I

Rule 17

II

(ii) WHEN BOTH HAVE THE WIND ON THE SAME SIDE, THE VESSEL WHICH IS TO WINDWARD SHALL KEEP OUT OF THE WAY OF THE VESSEL WHICH IS TO LEEWARD.

(b) FOR THE PURPOSES OF THIS RULE THE WINDWARD SIDE SHALL BE DEEMED TO BE THE SIDE OPPOSITE TO THAT ON WHICH THE MAINSAIL IS CARRIED OR, IN THE CASE OF A SQUARE-RIGGED VESSEL, THE SIDE OPPOSITE TO THAT ON WHICH THE LARGEST FORE-AND-AFT SAIL IS CARRIED.

The last bit, about square-rigged vessels, doesn't matter very much, but the rest is most important!

Rule 18 describes the action to be taken when two power-driven vessels are meeting end on. (Each shall alter course to starboard—i.e. 'keep to the right'.)

Rule 19 describes the action to be taken when two power-driven vessels are crossing so as to involve risk of collision.

Rule 20 This describes the action to be taken when a power-driven vessel and a sailing vessel are proceeding in such a way as to involve a risk of collision. (Except in certain circumstances, detailed elsewhere in the Rules, the power-driven vessel, being the more manœuvrable, shall keep out of the way of the sailing vessel.)

Rule 21 lays down that the vessel which has the right of way shall maintain her course and speed, unless collision is imminent.

Rule 22 lays down that any vessel which has to give way shall take avoiding action as soon as she can, and shall if possible avoid crossing ahead of the other.

Rule 23 lays down that any vessel which has to give way shall, if necessary, slacken speed, stop, or go astern.

Rule 24 lays down that every overtaking vessel, whether she is power-driven or under sail, shall keep out of the way of the vessel she is overtaking.

Rule 25 lays down the behaviour required of power-driven vessels in narrow channels.

Rule 26 lays down that all vessels not engaged in fishing shall keep out of the way of those which are.

Rule 27 is concerned with special considerations which may affect the steering and Sailing Rules in general.

Four other rules complete the 'seaway code' :

Rule 28 lays down the sound signals to be made by one vessel when manœuvring within sight of another.

Rule 29 is a general one, laying down the necessity of efficient and seamanlike conduct of the vessel at all times.

Rule 30 states that the 'Rules' in general may be modified by special local rules laid down by local authorities.

Rule 31 is concerned with distress signals. The rule enumerates eleven distress signals in all, the last two of which are of special interest to small boat sailors because of their simplicity. These are :

'(x) A smoke signal giving off a volume of orange coloured smoke.'

'(xi) Slowly and repeatedly raising and lowering arms outstretched to each side.'

Let us hope you will never have to use either !

Some of the rules in Code are more honoured by yachtsmen in the breach than in the observance. I have yet to see, for instance, a yacht exhibiting the appropriate day signal (a black, conical shape, point downwards) when she is proceeding under sail and power (Rule 14). Some yachtsmen, too, especially if they are inexperienced, may decide to keep out of the way of a larger vessel, even when they have the right of way, and there is nothing wrong with this *so long as avoiding action is taken in ample time, well before the other vessel is likely to initiate the course of action required of her in a collision situation.*

In many coastal areas it is possible for small craft, by avoiding deep-water channels, to make a passage without encountering commercial shipping at all, and the men aboard these ships will say nothing but 'thank you' to you for this. But this does not absolve you from knowing the rule of the road, because where you can go, other small craft can go too. A collision with another craft of your own size may not be so disastrous as one with a ship, but it may still be damaging, and demoralising, and an unseamanlike thing to happen. It should never happen!

To sum up : Get the Rules, read them, and note the points in them which are most likely to concern you. The craft you will most frequently encounter when you are under way, and particularly when you are starting off from or returning to your base, will be other yachts, so you should familiarise yourself with Rule 17 until you know it so well that you automatically know what course of action you should take in any collision situation. Then you will be safe—so long as the man in the other boat knows Rule 17 too!

9

Safety at Sea

ONE thing above all others should be constantly borne in mind about the sea: *It can drown you.* (It can also, of course, drown anybody else aboard.) Less dramatically, it can cause damage to your yacht and her equipment, or injury to her complement.

Remember that most accidents at sea are caused by ignorance or carelessness; and that when such accidents happen, not only your yacht and those aboard her may be imperilled, but so may other craft and the people in them, to say nothing of the risk to the craft and lives of others attempting to render assistance.

It is up to the owner-skipper to ensure, as far as it lies within his power to do so, that no such accidents ever happen. If he has a proper sense of his responsibilities he will take every possible precaution against all foreseeable eventualities.

What are these eventualities?

Some of the safeguards detailed below are self-evident, and some have been noted before. But safety at sea is so important that no apology is necessary for stressing them or mentioning them again.

First of all your yacht must be thoroughly sound and all her gear completely reliable.

Hull

The yacht's hull must be known to be sound. If you buy a second-hand craft, a professional survey is important not only as an aid to valuation but as an assurance of safety, and the condition of the hull will obviously be a major item on the survey report.

The hull must also be properly maintained after purchase, and if at any time it appears that it may have suffered damage or strain—perhaps after taking the ground heavily—it should be carefully inspected by someone who knows what he is about, perhaps by the local boat yard, or even by a professional surveyor again. It is not good enough to say, 'She leaks a bit more since she ran on, but it only means a few more strokes on the pump.'

Spars, rigging, sails

The yacht's spars, standing and running rigging, and sails must be sound. The condition of her standing rigging is most important to her safety, and it is vital that this should not be overlooked when the yacht is surveyed. This can happen if the rigging in question is tucked away in some shed or other when the yacht is laid up.

Repairs to and replacements of standing rigging should be put into the hands of a boat yard, or at least of someone experienced in this kind of work. There are two reasons for this: (1) standing rigging is wire, and wire splicing will be beyond the capacity of the inexperienced yachtsman; (2) getting the right length for the wires concerned, and setting standing rigging up correctly, is a professional job.

Some replacements of running rigging can be undertaken by the beginner—making and reeving a new mainsheet, or new jib sheets, for example; but here again he probably won't be able to tackle anything involving wire.

Auxiliary engine

The auxiliary engine, if the yacht has one, *must* be reliable.

An engine which won't always start when it is needed, or one which may pack up without warning, can be worse than none at all.

Engines are particularly important nowadays, in all but the smallest yachts, for entering and leaving harbour. Many yacht anchorages are now so crowded that, whether we like it or not, it is virtually impossible, or at best an inconsiderate thing to do, to try to get in or out of them under sail. An engine failure at such times may not have the most dire results, but it can cost quite a lot in terms of loss of paint and popularity!

The unreliability of yacht engines, or at any rate of those in older craft, is a standing joke with many yachtsmen. It isn't much of a joke really.

Fire and explosion

If you have a petrol engine and/or a bottled gas or paraffin cooker, you have danger aboard. Make absolutely certain that the petrol tank, gas cylinder, etc., does not leak, and that all fuel lines are sound, and properly supported and jointed. Be very careful when filling fuel tanks aboard, particularly the fuel tank of your auxiliary engine, to avoid spillage which may get down into the bilges. Maintain all engines, stoves, lamps, etc., in a clean and efficient condition.

Accidents of this kind should never happen—but they do. I know one man whose stove blew up and set fire to his yacht one evening when he and his wife were preparing supper, while the yacht was on her mooring. The yachtsman and his lady had to abandon ship and swim for it, and ended up on opposite banks of the river in which the yacht was lying. The yacht was a total write-off. The yachtsman was a humorous fellow and made an amusing tale out of it all later, but, again, this can't have been very funny really. And it would have been a lot less so if it had happened at sea.

It is a wise precaution to carry aboard at least one fire extinguisher, of the small type suitable for yachts. A good

stowage for this in a yacht with a normal layout would be
on the bulkhead at the after end of the cabin, where it would
be convenient to the most likely sources of fire.

Ground tackle

A friend and I, when visiting the Daily Express Boat Show
a year or two back, were admiring a gleaming new yacht of
eight tons or so when we noticed that something was missing.
There was no navel pipe to lead the anchor chain below.
Nor was there any fairlead for the chain over the bows. On
inquiry, we found that no provision at all had been made
for the yacht to anchor.

Such an omission is so absurd as to be almost incredible.
An anchor or anchors (plus cable, or line) are most important items of any yacht's, and particularly of a cruising yacht's,
equipment. When cruising, you may want to drop the hook
for all sorts of reasons, from 'staying put' in fog or holding
your vessel off some danger she is being set on to (perhaps
because your engine has failed!) to nothing more than having
lunch in peace and quiet. The ability to anchor is particularly
important to the cruising novice, who probably won't be on
the go all the time, and who, specifically, is unlikely to be
doing much night sailing. If he wants to lie overnight in some
lonely creek or other he will have to lie to an anchor, as he
will also have to do in many yacht harbours, unless he is
lucky enough to pick up a mooring and stay on it (if he
picks up a visitors' mooring he should be all right, but if he
is on a private one, and the owner comes back later, he will
have to move).

A yacht of any size at all will in all probability carry two
anchors—a large one, called the 'bower' anchor, and a small
one, known as a kedge. The large one will be carried on the
fore-deck, with a length of chain (properly called cable)
fastened at one end to the ring of the anchor and leading
down through the navel pipe (which is, basically, an aper-
ture in the fore-deck) to the fore-peak, or 'cable locker',
where the other, inboard, end should be secured. If it isn't,

and you throw your anchor overboard with gay abandon—
which you shouldn't do anyway—your anchor and cable may
lay themselves on the sea-bed and be lost for good, and serve
you right!

The kedge anchor will normally be used with a line, not
cable, and such an anchor is carried primarily for temporary
use. Since a kedge, plus its line, will be much lighter than
the bower anchor, plus its cable, it will be handier to use
for short 'stops'—as in some of the instances quoted above.
It should never be used when the yacht is going to be left
unattended, or for an overnight stop, which amounts to much
the same thing.

The large anchor, being your most reliable means of
staying in one place, should be ready for use at all times, and
this is why it is carried on the fore-deck, with its cable attached and ready to run out (you should make sure, incidentally, that it *is* free to run up from below, and can't foul
anything in the fore-peak). The kedge, since it will be used
only occasionally, and then not often, in cases of emergency,
and because it is light enough to be easily portable, may be
stowed away in some convenient place below decks, either
with or without its line attached.

It is, of course, vital that your bower anchor and cable
should be adequate to hold your yacht under any reasonable
weather conditions. This holding power will depend on (a)
the weight and design of the anchor; (b) the strength of the
cable, and how much of it you have veered.

We have mentioned the *design* of the anchor because this

Anchors

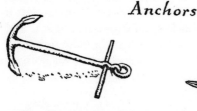

Fisherman's

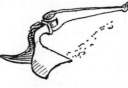

C.Q.R

materially affects its holding power. The traditional anchor, one with which everyone must surely be familiar, is that known as the fisherman's anchor (see page 121). This consists essentially of a shank with a curved bar at the bottom terminating in two flukes, and a stock or crosspiece at the top which acts as a trip-bar to bring one or the other of the flukes into the right position to dig into the sea-bed. In comparatively recent years, however, another design of anchor, known as the C.Q.R. anchor (page 121) has been rapidly gaining popularity, and with good reason. The C.Q.R. anchor, which, as can be seen from the illustration, is shaped like a ploughshare, has much greater holding power, weight for weight, than a fisherman's anchor, and therefore a lighter anchor can be used.

Also, with a C.Q.R., there is much less chance of a yacht fouling her anchor and pulling it out. This is most likely to happen when, as the yacht rides up over her anchor—usually when the tide turns—her cable gets foul of it. This is obviously an ever-present possibility with the fisherman's anchor, since one of the two flukes will almost always be sticking up from the sea-bed, whereas the same situation will not exist with a C.Q.R.

Anchoring

Anchoring is a procedure which will be new to most people who are coming to cruising for the first time, either direct or from dinghy sailing, so we ought perhaps to take a look at it. It is also appropriate in a chapter on sea safety, since a yacht which drags her anchor in a creek or harbour can cause a lot of damage, both to herself and possibly to other craft too. If she has dropped her hook in an emergency at sea, and it fails to hold, the consequences can be still more serious.

There are four main considerations when anchoring, at least if you are going to stay put for any length of time (say, overnight). These are :

1. Choose as sheltered a spot as possible, allowing for possible shifts of the wind.

2. Make sure there will be enough depth of water there *at low water* for you to remain afloat (unless you have the sort of yacht which will happily take the ground, and you are happy for her to do so).

3. You should veer (let out) sufficient cable for your yacht to ride safely to her anchor *at high water*. This means that normally you should veer not less than three times the depth at that spot at high water; a large part of the holding power of a yacht's ground tackle comes from that part of her cable which lies along the sea-bed, and a horizontal pull will make the anchor hold more effectively, whereas, if you veer too little cable, the pull on the anchor may be upwards, and this may break it out.

4. When anchoring, you should concern yourself not so much with where the anchor will be lying as with where the yacht will be when she is lying to it; she must be free to swing without the danger of striking any hazards in the vicinity, including other craft.

There is also the question of what length of anchor cable you will need. This may be governed to some extent by what sort of waters you are sailing in, and on the size of your craft. Bearing in mind that you should veer a length equal to three times the maximum depth at the spot where you

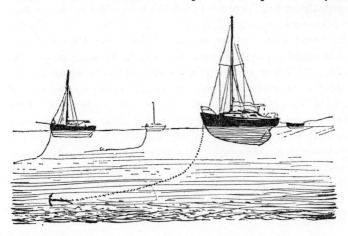

will be lying, thirty fathoms of cable will enable you to anchor
in depths of up to about ten fathoms, which will probably
be more than deep enough for the beginner's purposes, even
with a five-tonner. Smaller, shallower-draught yachts sailing
in shoal areas, will be able to make do with proportionately
less.

Bearing in mind the possibility of an emergency, or perhaps an excursion into deeper waters than usual, you should
not skimp yourself over cable. If you can manage it, you
should carry a rather greater length than you are likely to
need.

You should also mark your cable at intervals—the best
way is by painting a link, or links, preferably white—as a
guide to how much you have veered. The intervals at which
you mark your cable, and how you mark it, is up to you.
One method, and a good one, is to paint one link for every
'unit'—say every five fathoms—veered. With this method,
three consecutive painted links will mean you have veered
fifteen fathoms of cable; and so on.

Coming to anchor

When coming to anchor, you should so manœuvre your
yacht that all the way will be off her when she is over the
spot where the anchor is to lie. Wait until she begins to drop
back—inshore, you will usually be able to check this by lining
up visual marks in the vicinity. Then lower your anchor—
don't hurl it over the bows. You can be as smart as you like
about letting it go, but you should control its descent, if for
no other reason that if you let the cable rush out, you *could*
get a turn round an ankle, or step on it, either of which
could have unfortunate results; or the cable could snag somewhere, with resultant damage. In any case, if you do not
pay out your cable, but let it run out, you will not be able to
control how much you are veering, and you may have to
haul some of it in again, which will be work for nothing.
There is plenty of hard work about a yacht without looking
for more.

When you have veered the correct amount of cable, turn it up on the samson post. Then check, again by your visual marks, that the anchor is holding; and make sure, too, that you have correctly estimated your yacht's position, with reference both to other craft and hazards such as buoys, jetties, etc., and that she will be able to swing freely. When you have done this, you can go below for your gin with an easy mind.

Now let us look at some of the other safety precautions which can be taken :

Staying aboard

A major and ever-present danger with a small yacht is that of someone falling overboard. If the yacht is at anchor, or on a mooring, this may result in nothing worse than a wetting for the person concerned—though a yachting acquaintance of mine was drowned in this way within a few feet of his yacht when she was on her home mooring, because he could not swim. A strong tide and/or darkness may also seriously complicate such a situation, even if the person *can* swim. And if the mishap occurs when a yacht is under way at sea, a grave emergency will almost always result. Even in daylight and good weather conditions, it can be surprisingly difficult to spot someone in the water, and unless the correct course of action is taken, and taken immediately, some little time and a good deal of confusion may ensue before the yacht can be put about and brought back to pick up the casualty, by which time it may be too late.

The correct 'man overboard' drill will be detailed later in this chapter. For the moment let us concentrate on staying on board, which, after all, is the best drill of all. Prevention is better than cure, and this is truer at sea than almost anywhere else.

Many yachts nowadays, except some of the smallest, where it is not practicable, have the deck 'fenced round'. This 'fence' usually consists of a rigid construction at the bows, wire guard rails along the sides, and sometimes, but less frequently, another rigid construction at the stern.

Pulpit : This is the name given to the construction at the bows, which is normally made of metal piping. This provides a measure of protection, and also provides a possible 'anchor point' (see later) for anyone working on the fore-deck. Protection is needed here, because a good deal has to be done on the fore-deck (chiefly changing headsails), often in lively conditions, and anyone working here is in a very vulnerable and insecure position.

Pushpit : The rigid construction aft is known by humorous analogy with that at the bows, as a 'pushpit'. Pushpits are much less commonly found than pulpits, for the very good reason that they are not so necessary to safety aboard. Aft, on most small yachts anyway, most if not all the procedures necessary when under way can be done from the comparative safety of the cockpit.

Guard rails : Guard rails are made of wire, supported at intervals by stanchions. They are not feasible on some very small yachts because they would obstruct movement fore and aft on deck; to be more specific, they would leave insufficient width of side-deck for movement past the cabin top (and doghouse, if there is one).

On yachts on which guard rails can be fitted it is important that these should be *high* enough to fulfil their intended function. I have seen yachts on which the guard rail along each side consisted of a single wire running a foot or less above deck-level. Such a wire may easily prove to be a trip wire rather than anything else, and 'guard rails' of this kind will therefore be a hazard rather than a safeguard. In my opinion guard rails should be at least two feet high if they are to do what they are meant to do.

Safety harness : One way of ensuring that you stay *with*

the yacht, even if you don't stay *on* her, is to wear a safety harness. This consists essentially of a belt to which is attached a line with a snap hook or similar fitting by which you can hook yourself on to a suitable part of the yacht.

P. J. Haward, who spends a lot of his time ferrying yachts of all kinds to all sorts of places, and who therefore has great experience of being at sea in small craft, was one of the pioneers of this kind of equipment, and his own design of safety belt is probably in wider use today, in British waters anyway, than any other. This harness consists of a belt to which is attached a line which can be used at two alternative lengths, one short and one long.

Your first reaction to the idea of wearing a safety harness

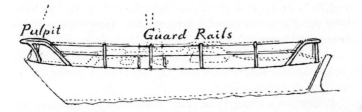

may be a reluctance to do so on the grounds that it will restrict your movements too much, but it is surprising how quickly you can get used to one. If you wear one when you are at the helm—which is sometimes most advisable, for under certain conditions it is not at all difficult to get washed out of a yacht's cockpit, particularly if it is a shallow one —you may, to start with, particularly after a spell of going about fairly frequently, end up bound hand and foot, but once you have got the knack of things, this will sort itself out. In fact after you have worn a safety harness regularly for some time you will scarcely notice it at all, other than as a comforting thing to have around (you).

You will, of course, need more than one 'anchor point' if you move from one end of the yacht to the other, but the normal yacht will provide plenty of these, and the 'scope' of the harness will be such that you will not need to re-anchor yourself very often.

To sum up on this point: It is better to put up with a little restriction on board than to fall over the side with full and perfect freedom to wave your yacht goodbye.

It is more important to wear a safety harness at night than during the day, since the consequences of going over the side are likely to be much more serious during the hours of darkness. Similarly, it is more important to wear one when you are sailing single-handed than when you have other people aboard.

Man overboard!

If someone does fall overboard when the yacht is under way, and he is lucky enough not to be sailing alone and to have someone else see or hear him go, the following steps must be taken, and taken at once:

1. If possible, a lifebuoy or some other buoyant object should be thrown over the side, as near to the person in the water as can be managed.

2. Someone aboard the yacht should keep a constant eye on the victim. Once he has been lost sight of, it may, as we have said earlier, be very difficult to spot him again.

3. If the yacht is proceeding under sail the helmsman must gybe her. Whatever the weather conditions, and whatever the yacht's point of sailing, *she must be gybed*. Even if in certain circumstances this may in itself be an unseamanlike thing to do, such a consideration will be automatically outweighed by the fact that a life may well be at stake. By gybing, the yacht will be brought as quickly as possible into a position to be leeward of the person in the water from which she can be brought up to him head to wind and therefore under control, able to check her speed to pick him up. If you go roaring down upon him from windward you can easily either miss him altogether, because of your inability to check your speed, or run him down.

A crowd of small cruising craft in the harbour at Scarborough, Yorks

The end of a perfect day – and what will tomorrow be like?

Lifejackets, etc.

Supposing you are unfortunate enough to find yourself in the water, unattached to your yacht, the thing that may tip the balance between whether you sink or swim may well be a lifebelt, or lifejacket.

This brings us to three points of primary importance where safety at sea is concerned :

1. There must be a lifebelt or lifejacket for everyone on board.

2. These belts or jackets must be of a design, strength, and buoyancy to perform their function properly.

3. These vital items of equipment must be stowed (when they are not being worn) in a place or places everyone knows about, and where they will be immediately available.

So many makes and designs of lifebelt and lifejacket exist nowadays, from the old Board of Trade back-and-front kapok pads to the most sophisticated garments, that it is difficult to single out any particular model. This is something you should take advice on, and, presuming this, it is enough for us to emphasise the two major requirements of a belt or jacket. These are :

1. That it will provide sufficient buoyancy for the wearer, even if he is unconscious and therefore unable to help himself at all.

2. That it will support the body—again, even in unconsciousness—in an attitude which will keep the head, and particularly the face, well clear of the water.

The designs most favoured today are lifejackets rather than lifebelts, and these have the added advantage that they provide protection against the weather when worn aboard. Many a yachtsman who is not over-concerned for his safety will wear a lifejacket for comfort, particularly at night; which is a good thing, since he will then be provided with a safety factor in spite of himself, and at a time when he may need it most.

Lifejackets should be of a colour which can be easily picked

I

out in the sea. Bright yellow or orange are the best in this respect, and are therefore the most common.

Abandon ship!

(Let's hope you will never come to it. But you might. At sea you must be prepared for anything!)

Dinghy into lifeboat: An occasion could arise when it will be necessary for you to leave your yacht because otherwise she will leave you—for example, if she was foundering, breaking up, or on fire. These are extreme situations, and should never happen—but, as we have just said, they could!

Under such circumstances your dinghy will become your lifeboat. Unfortunately the ordinary small wooden, or rigid, dinghy is far from seaworthy in really bad conditions. An inflatable rubber dinghy is an infinitely better lifeboat, and this may well be worth thinking about by anyone who has yet to buy a tender to his yacht.

If you already have, or acquire, a rubber dinghy you should make sure that it will fulfil the function required of it. You should take care to observe the following precautions :

1. If the dinghy is carried below make sure it is stowed somewhere where you can get at it without removing most of the contents of the yacht first.

2. If you do not use it often, check regularly that it will inflate—i.e. that it is not holed, that its valve or valves work, and that the appropriate inflating mechanism exists and is in good working order.

Remember, too, that the material of which such a dinghy is made is perishable and that it will therefore not have a very long serviceable life. You should be quite certain that it is in good condition, and the only way to do this is to have it inspected at reasonable intervals by the makers, or at any rate by someone who really knows about this kind of craft.

Liferafts

The best lifeboat of all for small craft is an inflatable rubber

raft, of the kind which is specifically intended for survival
at sea. Such a raft is equipped with a cover, which greatly
increases its seaworthiness and also provides invaluable protection for the occupants. A liferaft of this kind will usually
be provided with both automatic and 'stand by' (manual)
means of inflation, plus distress signals and other stores and
resources.

Liferafts are, however, essentially *rafts*, not boats. Circular
in shape, they are not practicable for use as tenders, and
since few small yachts can afford the space to carry two
boats, they are not commonly found aboard small craft; or
not unless the owner of the yacht in question is more than
normally preoccupied with safety precautions.

Bad weather

The rather grim theme we have been pursuing above leads
us naturally to the subject of bad weather and what to do
about it.

The question immediately poses itself: what is bad weather
from the cruising yachtsman's point of view? And the initial
answer is, as it must be to so many sailing questions, *it all
depends*.

It depends, in fact, on many things, e.g. on whether you
are in harbour or at sea when the 'dirt' develops; on how
long a passage you are making, or planning to make; on
what sort of waters you are or will be sailing through; on
what harbours or sheltered waters you can seek refuge in, if
necessary; on whether you will have a fair wind or not (even
if it is half a gale); on what, if you *do* decide to make a bid
to reach your destination, the state of the tide will be when
you get there; on the competence and experience of the complement of your yacht (including yourself); and so on.

You should take particular note of the direction of the
wind. If it is blowing onshore will you have dangers under
your lee? You should never risk being caught by really heavy
weather on a lee shore. If it is offshore what will it be like
'outside'? It is easy to underestimate the strength of a wind

I*

blowing off the land, because the sea under the lee of the land may be fairly calm. Being blown out to sea may be better than being set on a lee shore, but this too is a thing to be avoided!

Suppose you are in a harbour and the weather deteriorates before departure time comes for the passage you have planned, what do you do?

Presuming that conditions are not impossible, that the weather is not likely to get worse, that the waters you will be sailing through offer no grave dangers in such weather, *and* that you can get out of *and back into* the harbour where you are now lying without hazard, the golden rule is to *go out and have a look*. Conditions may be better outside than you thought, and after you have got the feel of it out there you may feel confident enough to proceed. Even if you have to come back in again you will at least have had a go, and your nautical honour will be vindicated. Most people have only a limited time for sailing, and there is nothing more frustrating than to have the weather fair up just after you've missed the tide which you needed to catch to get you to the destination you had planned for that week-end. Nor is there anything more annoying and humiliating than to have someone who did go out to look, and who then pressed on, come back and bore you in the club with what a wonderful trip he had!

Besides, you will find that, once you have put off making a start, it is extraordinary easy to go on putting it off, and you may end up by not moving off your mooring. You sit there, wishing you were braver. Demoralisation sets in, with consequent discord aboard, at home, and at the office during the ensuing week! It's all very bad indeed for the morale.

A word of caution, though. Before going out to see what things are like outside, make absolutely sure you *will* be able to get in again. Think what it will be like coming back. For example, suppose you leave harbour on the top of a tide, with a strong onshore wind blowing. You get out all right, but after a while you decide you must turn back. By the time you reach the harbour entrance again, the ebb may be running strongly against the wind, building up an ugly sea.

And again : Confidence is an entirely different thing from foolhardiness. If you go out to look at the weather you should decide to proceed only if you are sure it will be safe for you to do so. You must always assess the situation as well as you can, in as many of its aspects as possible. You must know what the weather, your boat and those aboard her are capable of doing. You should never be reckless or impulsive. I vividly remember two people leaving harbour in a Folkboat in very bad conditions for no better reason than that they had been weatherbound for three days and the 'skipper' had got fed up with it. I was sitting on a mooring in the cockpit of my own yacht and as he passed me he called out, with a note of despair in his voice, 'It's just not on !' And it wasn't. I've not seen him or his boat since, but I've often wondered what happened to him.

Weather forecasting

In any kind of fight we need to know as much about our opponent as possible, and sailing is essentially a fight against wind and sea.

Earlier in this book we saw the importance of getting to know one's sailing ground as intimately as possible, and also got some idea of the sources from which such knowledge can be acquired. Getting to know about the weather, and what sort of conditions to expect at sea, is a less easy study, because there is nothing really hard-and-fast to go on. At the same time, we can learn to forecast pretty well what sort of weather is likely to develop in the near future—even if it doesn't !

Broadcast weather forecasts are, of course, invaluable to the yachtsman, and for this reason, if for no other, every yacht should have a radio aboard. The ordinary 'shoreside' radio—one of the ubiquitous transistor portables, for example —is however, far from ideal for use afloat (though it will be a lot better than none at all) because of its vulnerability to damage and damp. You would be much better advised, if you can run to it, to buy one of the more rugged sets which are specially designed for use at sea.

A D.F. set is not a necessity for the cruising novice, but there is, of course, no reason why he shouldn't invest in such a set if he had a particular interest in this sort of apparatus. A D.F. radio will increase in usefulness as he extends the range of his cruising, and any early practice he may get in using it for navigational purposes will be invaluable later on.

Weather systems

Two terms very commonly used in radio forecasts may be mentioned here : (1) anti-cyclone; (2) depression.

Anti-cyclone : This is a weather system in which winds blow clockwise around an area of high pressure. An anti-cyclone is a fair-weather system which, fortunately, often lasts quite a while. Anti-cyclonic winds are of moderate strength and, generally speaking, anti-cyclones bring yachtsmen's weather.

Depression : This is a weather system in which winds blow anticlockwise around an area of low pressure. Depressions bring high winds and rain, and for a lot of us mean 'clubhouse weather'. A depression may not last very long but it is frequently followed by others, which may add up to a long period of poor or bad conditions.

Barometer

The other essential item of weather-forecasting equipment is a barometer, which will always give warning of significant meteorological changes, even if its behaviour is sometimes open to alternative interpretations.

The barometer is simply an instrument for measuring atmospheric pressure. A high reading will normally mean fine weather and a low reading bad weather. A *slowly* rising barometer means that there will be less wind and rain, while a *slowly* falling barometer will mean more of both. Any *rapid* rise or fall in barometric pressure will mean that a sudden change is taking place, and that therefore unsettled weather is on the way.

Cloud formations, etc.

Much can also be predicted from the 'look' of the weather, and particularly from clouds. There is a lot to be learned here, and even then it is possible to be wrong quite often. A weather situation can change suddenly in an unexpected way. At the same time if we know how to interpret the 'sky-signs' above us, we can reasonably expect to be right more often than not.

There are four main types of cloud : (1) cirrus; (2) cumulus; (3) stratus; (4) nimbus.

Cirrus : This is the 'thread' cloud. It is high cloud, and is sometimes called 'mares' tails'. Isolated threads of cirrus may occur in fine weather. If they grow to cover an increasing area of the sky and become more regular in formation, bad weather is probably on the way.

Cumulus : This, as its name indicates, is a 'heap' cloud. Isolated, fairly small cumulus clouds are fair-weather clouds. Many of us must have enjoyed being at sea on days when these balls of cotton wool have been sailing across a blue sky, all of them more or less the same height, and brilliant white in a sun that never seems to go in. This is real 'yachtsman's weather'.

Cumulus clouds are formed by upward currents of air. If they get bigger this means that the air currents are becoming more violent, and a change in the weather can be expected.

Stratus : This is another self-explanatory term, stratus being a 'sheet' cloud. If stratus cloud spreads over the sky, it is likely that fairly prolonged rain will follow. The rain, will, however, not normally be heavy.

Nimbus: This is the grey, shapeless, sometimes ragged rain cloud with which we are all only too familiar. There is no need to predict when the bad weather will come. It's arrived!

The above kinds of cloud also occur in various combinations.

Cirro-cumulus: This is the high, 'bobbly' cloud which is sometimes called a 'mackerel' sky. Isolated patches occur in fine weather, but, as with cirrus, if this cloud spreads and becomes regular in formation, conditions will probably deteriorate.

Cirro-stratus: This is a thin, whitish veil of cloud which may again regularise as bad weather approaches.

Alto-cumulus: 'High' cumulus. This formation consists of rippled cloudlets, and occurs in fine weather.

Fracto-cumulus: 'Broken' cumulus. This means unsettled conditions.

Cumulo nimbus: This is stuff to beware of. It consists of large, towering masses of cloud, very dark on the underside because the sun cannot get through. Because of its mass, such a cloud will have an enormous water-vapour content, which means it may bring heavy rain, squalls, hail, and lightning.

Strato-cumulus: This is a sheet of small-scale cumulus. If it spreads to cover the sky it means wind is on the way.

Fracto-stratus: Broken stratus. This is sometimes preceded by cirro-stratus, and may develop into grey alto-stratus. A 'watery' sun will be visible, perhaps with a halo round it. In all likelihood rain is on the way.

There are all sorts of ways of estimating what the weather

is likely to do, some of them 'scientific', some of them home-spun. To take one or two instances at random, a 'backing' wind—i.e. one which shifts its direction anticlockwise, means conditions will probably deteriorate; if a blow comes on suddenly it probably won't last long; a wind off the sea is more likely to bring rain than a wind off the land; if the seabirds are sticking close to the coast you might be well advised to too. And so on. . . .

To sum up : To get some idea of what the weather is going to be like you should have a radio and a barometer, and keep your eyes and ears open. You should be able to pick up at least a few 'weather saws' from local fishermen, yachtsmen who have more experience than you and other such people whose business or pleasure has to do with the sea and its moods. If you are sensible, and careful, it is unlikely that you will ever be caught out by really bad weather.

One point remains to be made here. Most books on sailing, when discussing the subject, maintain that you should never run for harbour in really bad conditions unless you are sure you can get in safely. Instead, you should *stand out to sea*.

This, let me say at once, is good seamanlike advice, but it is perhaps asking rather a lot of the beginner. Its validity, for him, depends upon his ability to handle his craft—and also, of course, on the seaworthiness of the craft herself. Then again, what does standing out to sea involve? It depends a good deal on where you are. It would be a much easier or at least a much more straightforward thing to do off a deep-water coast, where there are no dangers, than it would be in a shoal area such as the Thames Estuary, with its innumerable banks.

Bad weather doesn't usually develop so quickly that the 'short haul' cruising man won't be able to find shelter somewhere, and the best rule for the beginner is that he should make as sure as he can that he will be able to do this. Later on when he is more experienced, he can sample the delights of heaving to and all the rest of it.

What other precautions should be taken to ensure safety at sea?

Radar reflector

Nowadays most ships are equipped with radar—which, while it undoubtedly is a boon to them, can be quite the reverse to small craft sailing in the same waters. It means that large vessels can now charge ahead in fog or other murky conditions at speeds which would be impossible without this aid, and the danger here is that most yachts are not only so low on the water as to be difficult to spot but are in many cases constructed of materials which do not 'reflect' on the radar screen.

The answer to this is the radar reflector, which is a metal 'shape' which can be hoisted in conditions of limited visibility. (Such a reflector is a cheap and simple piece of equipment which can easily be stowed below when not in use.)

If carried aboard, a radar reflector should always be hoisted at night, even in clear weather, since a small yacht's running lights are not usually powerful enough and may not be carried high enough to be seen at any great distance. For this reason too the helmsman should always have a torch to hand—the more powerful the better—which he can shine on the sails of his yacht in any situation which seems to require it.

Fog

In addition to taking common-sense precautions such as keeping out of channels used by shipping (if this is possible) a yacht, if she is to comply with the Collision Regulations, should have some means of making her presence known audibly.

Rule 15 of the Regulations specifies that a sailing vessel of over forty feet in length shall carry a foghorn and bell. Such a vessel shall sound, at intervals of not more than one minute, one blast when on the starboard tack, two blasts in succession when on the port tack, and three blasts in succession when she is running with the wind abaft the beam. When at anchor, she shall ring the bell rapidly for five seconds at intervals of not more than one minute.

The Rule goes on to say that a craft of less than forty feet in length is not obliged to give these signals, but, if she does not, must make 'some other efficient sound signal' at intervals of not more than one minute.

Radar Reflector

For the yachtsman, a simple mouth-operated foghorn will be the best means of making the necessary sound signals when under way. And if you want to advertise your presence at anchor you can make a very satisfactory clatter by beating a frying-pan or some such utensil with something suitably hard.

Flares

Every cruising yacht should carry distress signals. For the

small vessel doing short coastal trips, a box of flares will do. In most situations these will be adequate to draw the attention of another vessel, or of people on shore.

Setting off a flare or flares is also a means of warning another vessel of the danger of collision—a last-resort means, perhaps, but an effective one.

Flares should be supplied in a sealed container. You should know how to use them, and also check from time to time that they are in a suitable condition. If the sealing of the container remains intact, they should not deteriorate.

First aid
Every yacht should carry a first-aid box, and every yacht skipper should have at least an elementary knowledge of what to do in cases of sickness or injury. This knowledge should include artificial respiration.

Seasickness:
Anything which reduces a yachtsman's efficiency is a danger, not only to him but to everyone else, and seasickness certainly does this.

Seasickness prevention has made great strides in the last quarter of a century, chiefly because it was an important aspect of many operations in World War II. Nowadays a number of highly effective treatments exist. But they don't all of them suit everyone. If you and those who sail with you suffer in this way it is worth experimenting to find out which of the various treatments available will control your queaziness best, and, which is also very important, impair your efficiency least.

Watch-keeping
It is most important when sailing that every 'operative' person aboard should keep as fresh and alert as possible, and this is best achieved by a sensible division of duties. Many owner-skippers tend to run the whole show themselves, or they try to, and wear themselves out, while the rest of the

'crew' get bored through having too little to do. This is not at all a desirable state of affairs, since both having too much or too little to do can result in a loss of efficiency.

The apportioning of specific duties—navigation, cooking, etc., will depend upon what sort of complement the yacht has. Allowing for this, it is a good idea that some sort of watch-keeping system should be observed, the length of the watches and the frequency of their recurrence being dependent upon how many persons there are aboard who are competent to stand a watch. Even on a lazy cruise, when little sailing is done and a lot of time is spent at anchor, it is desirable that there should always be a definite person at least nominally on watch.

The naval system of watches divides the twenty-four hours of the day into seven watches, five of them of four hours each, and two of them of two hours each (these two are known as the dog-watches). The actual division is as follows :

Midnight — 4 a.m.	Middle watch
4 a.m. — 8 a.m.	Morning watch
8 a.m. — 12 noon	Forenoon watch
12 noon — 4 p.m.	Afternoon watch
4 p.m. — 6 p.m.	First dog-watch
6 p.m. — 8 p.m.	Second dog-watch
8 p.m. — 12 p.m.	First watch

The division of the four hours between 4 p.m. amd 8 p.m. into two two-hour watches results in there being an odd number of watches in the twenty-four-hour cycle, and this means that the watchkeeping system is staggered—i.e. that the same members of the crew won't keep the same watches on any two consecutive days.

Some such system of watchkeeping is desirable aboard a yacht, but at the same time the four-hour naval watch may be too long for many small-boat sailors, or for responsibility to be fairly divided if the passage is a very short one. It really all depends on how many of you there are, on what you are doing, and how rugged you are. For example, on a small yacht making a night passage with a crew of two, four hours at the tiller may be rather a strain, but on the other hand it will give the other chap a chance to get a decent bit of sleep. If there are more than two of you the watches can be shorter.

It is important, too, that, though someone else may be temporarily in command of the yacht, there must always be a skipper aboard; i.e. there must be someone—it will usually be the owner—whose orders *must* be obeyed by everyone else. For the skipper's part, it is up to him, in fairness to those who sail with him, to know what he is about, and to be able to implement his right of command. He should know, and make it quite precisely known, what he expects of the others as regards such things as the observance of safety regulations, the sailing of the ship, work aboard—and general behaviour aboard too.

Some—many—skippers are very lax in this respect. A few are very severe. I know one who insists that everyone who has a job to do on deck when his yacht is under way must wear a safety harness, whatever the weather. And who is to say he is wrong? After all, the safety of the crew is his responsibility.

In conclusion we will return very briefly to a subject which was discussed a good deal earlier in this book—the importance of proper food and sleep, etc. It is worth emphasising that these make for an efficient crew—and human efficiency aboard is every bit as important as a sound hull and gear. In fact the human element is the most easily exhausted or broken 'equipment' aboard. It is only common sense that it should be maintained at its peak strength and capacity.

10

The Yachting Year

MOST people who get the 'sailing bug' get it pretty badly, and this applies just as much to cruising types as it does to dinghy men. The infection is just as continuous, even if the period during which they are actually afloat is more clearly defined, and there are some months of apparent immunity during the winter.

The qualification 'apparent' is used above because during the months of the year when cruising yachtsmen are shore-bound, a good deal will still be going on, on foreshores or in boat yards—or in garages and gardens, if your yacht is one which you can trail home.

This shoreside activity will be at its most intense just after the end of one sailing season, and just before the next—in other words when you are laying up your yacht, and when you are fitting her out prior to her being put in the water again. But even in the depths of winter most of us will be doing *something*, even if it is nothing more than reading the yachting magazines, going to evening classes in navigation (not a bad idea), or dreaming in front of the fire about new gear—a new boat, even—and new ventures for the coming summer.

It is difficult, therefore, to say just when the yachting

season starts, because it doesn't really start at all. We shall therefore have to be a bit arbitrary about this—and, to be a bit Irish too, let us start when the actual sailing stops.

The question now arises—when should the sailing stop? Basically, this depends on you. You can go on sailing all the year round if you want to, doing your repair and maintenance work as and when you wish or can. (Whether you will be able to get anyone else to sail with you in January or February is another matter.) If you have a yacht which you can trail, you can take advantage of any good days or weekends that come along to dash down to the sea and get afloat. For most of us, however, the actual period when we can sail will have a definite beginning and a definite end.

One thing is worth mentioning here, and that is that, if you want to get the most you can out of a season, you should not be in too much of a hurry to lay up. Many people do this some time during September, but there is often good sailing weather in October. If this follows a bad summer, which has discouraged you so much that you have already had your yacht hauled out, you may feel cheated. The year 1965 was a case in point. A wretched summer was followed by some very good weather, in the south and east of Britain anyway, and many yachtsmen who had already packed it in for the season must have viewed those golden autumn days with a very jaundiced eye.

Laying up

The first practical question which arises when you are thinking of laying up your yacht is what sort of winter quarters do you want—or can you get—for her? This is presuming, of course, that you don't take her home.

Broadly speaking, there are three possibilities. You can leave her afloat. You can put her in a mud berth (if such exist and one is available at your base). You can have her hauled out and propped up on shore, either under a roof or out in the open.

Of the three, the first is not usually a very good idea. Your yacht will be exposed to too much stress of weather, she won't be easy to get to, and working aboard her will be more difficult than it need be. And she will have to be hauled out sooner or later anyway, to have her bottom done.

The second alternative is slightly to be preferred, in that she will be more protected in a mud berth, but she may still be difficult of access, and working aboard may not be easy. And again she will have to come out some time, for the same reason as above.

If you are planning to paint her topsides this won't be really practicable if she is lying afloat, even if she is afloat only at some states of the tide.

The third alternative is the best, namely to have her hauled out by the yacht yard, though it is not at all necessary for her to be put in a shed. Most yacht yards will have only very limited accommodation of this kind anyway, and what there is will probably be occupied by some of the fancier craft on the yard's books. Such storage will also be more expensive than storage in the open. (You will, of course, have to pay rent to the yard for storing your yacht. There will also be a charge for hauling her out; *and* for putting her in again next year.)

Either before or after the yacht actually leaves the water she will have to have her mast, or masts, removed. If she is of any size this will probably be a job for the yard, and they will do it at the stage of the operation which is most convenient for them. She will be de-rigged at the same time, and her guard rails, if any, will be removed too, though her pulpit may be left in place. She will then be struck over to the place she will occupy ashore during the winter.

She must now be covered over. A tarpaulin can be used for this purpose, but a proper boat cover is to be preferred, if you have one, or can afford to buy one. Such a cover will have a 'skirt' all round, which will help to keep the weather out and also protect her topsides.

The covering, whether it is a tarpaulin or a 'proper job', should be supported tent-fashion by a ridge-pole running

fore and aft along the centreline of the yacht (the yard will
provide this if you want them to). It is essential that the ends
of the 'tent' are left open to allow the free circulation of air.

Ventilation is extremely important, particularly below
decks, and particularly with a wooden boat. Locker doors
should be left open and the floorboards taken up. No compartment which can be opened up should be left shut, or not
for any length of time.

By this stage in the proceedings you will probably have
taken most of your gear off. You will no doubt be able to
store most if not all of the 'hardware' at the yard, but you
should take all 'perishables' home. These latter items include
bedding and bunk covers, navigational instruments, books
and charts, your radio, and perhaps your sails, though you
may decide to leave these with the sailmaker, if there is one
in the locality, for washing or repair. By the end of the season
your bedding, etc., will have become more or less impreg-
nated with salt, and this should be dealt with by washing or
dry-cleaning. Whether you do it yourself or not, sails should
be washed and dried and then carefully stored away.

Engine. The other major consideration as regards gear
will be your engine. If this is an outboard you can take it
home. Now is the time to have it serviced, and you can have
this done either by the makers or one of their agents, or by
your local garage. An inboard will have to be left where it
is—unless it has to come out for a complete overhaul or some
large-scale repair job—but it must not be neglected. The
engine itself should be drained and protected against rust.
The electrical equipment must be removed and stored. If
you are not particularly expert at or interested in this sort
of job yourself, it is one you can leave to the yacht yard.

Fuel tanks should be drained—no fuel or any kind should
be left on board. Batteries should be removed, serviced, and
stored.

You should leave your yacht as 'de-rigged' and empty as
possible. If she carries any inside ballast it should be removed.
The bilges should be cleaned.

The whole business of laying up should be done in a methodical manner. It will help a lot if you make an inventory of everything that is removed. All items of gear which are to be left at the yacht yard should be clearly labelled with the name of the yacht. To avoid any confusion or argument later, you should give the yard a duplicate list of these items.

Winter work

You should decide when you lay up, if not earlier, just what jobs you want the yard to do during the winter, at the same time bearing very much in mind what sort of bill you will be getting for it. The yard will almost certainly make a better fist of anything than you could, but remember that the amount of work you have done for you will materially affect your maintenance costs. Most yards have no objection to the yachtsman doing at least some of his own work—you will probably buy your paint and so on from them anyway. The wisest course, if you can afford it, is to leave to them anything that materially affects the yacht's seaworthiness, and which you don't feel entirely competent to tackle yourself. Standing rigging is a case in point. This will probably be a yard job. Such tasks as painting and varnishing you can undertake yourself. Your topsides would probably look glossier if the yard did them, but your safety at sea won't be affected.

Most yards like to have a bit of work to do on the yachts in their care. This is only natural. At the same time they won't thank you overmuch if, after letting things slide all winter, you give them a whole list of things you want done in the last week or two before the start of the new season. There are always too many people of this kind around, and the yard owner will greatly appreciate it if you tell him as soon as possible what you want done. He will then be able to fit the work in at slacker times, and the chances are that you will get a better job too. At least he won't have any excuse for not getting them done by the time you want to be

afloat again. Lack of consideration by yachtsmen in this respect causes more friction between them and yacht-yard
owners than anything else. The yard owner feels that you
have not given him a fair chance. And for your part there
is nothing more frustrating than to have a spot of good
weather come in right at the beginning of the new season,
and not to be able to take advantage of it because your yacht
is not in the water.

The same applies to gear which you have serviced elsewhere. If you want a sail repaired, or your compass over-
hauled, don't leave this to the last minute either. It is equally
annoying, even supposing that there is no delay in your getting afloat, not to be able to take advantage of that first
fine sailing day because your mainsail hasn't come back from
the sailmaker.

Once your yacht is properly laid up there will probably
be a lull in your nautical life, but the chances are that it
won't be long before you are tempted to go and have a look
at the old girl. If you do, it is a good idea to do a little more
than look. If it's a really nice fine day that has brought you
down, get the cover off her, or at least fold it back, so that
she can get a breath of air. And do some job or other, if you
can. However small it is, it will be one less to do later on.
Not only yacht yards but yacht owners too are apt to find
themselves with too much to do just before the new season
starts, and one reason that yacht yards get overburdened in
the spring is that some owners shift on to them at the last-
minute work they meant to do themselves, but didn't quite
get around to in time. Alternatively, some of these do-it-
yourself jobs may not get done at all. This, as we have said
earlier, probably won't affect the yacht's seaworthiness, but
she may not look so well as she might have done, and you
may not be quite so proud of her, or of yourself, as you could
have been.

It's useful if, when laying up, you not only tell the yard
what you want them to do, but also make a list of jobs for
yourself. Then you can tick them off as you do them, and

you will always have a pretty good idea of whether you are keeping ahead of the game or not. At the same time you should give some thought to the order in which you do these jobs. Some of them can be done at any time, but painting, for example, at any rate if the yacht is a wooden one, is best left to the spring, to give her a good chance to dry out. Varnishing is also a late job, because this should if possible be done on a fine, still, and reasonably warm day. In point of fact painting and varnishing will naturally come late in the programme, since you will want your yacht to look at her freshest when she takes the water again.

Fitting out

As spring comes on and the new season draws near, the tempo in the yacht yards will increase. More and more owners, their families and anyone else they can conscript into helping will be busy at the week-ends. Soon the first of the shored-up yachts will be going down the slip into the water, to be towed out to their moorings by the yard launch.

Now, again, you may be glad that you weren't in too much of a hurry to be hauled out at the end of last season. If yours was the first, or one of the first yachts out, she could have got tucked away in a corner of the yard where she would be hemmed in by other craft, and you might have to wait until they were afloat before your turn came. And if the yachts around yours were owned by dilatory types, your getting into the water could have been appreciably delayed.

Fitting out is essentially laying up in reverse. Gradually your gear gets back aboard—and this is when you realise how wise you were to make an inventory of everything, and to label those items which you left at the yard.

One of the last jobs to be done before your yacht is put back in the water is that of giving her bottom a coat of anti-fouling paint (she will have been scrubbed or scraped off when she was hauled out at the end of the previous season). This is a job which, unless you like making things difficult

K

for yourself, is best left to the yard. Anti-fouling is messy, and laborious to apply. Not only that—most kinds have to be put on within twenty-four hours of the yacht being launched. It will therefore be much more convenient for the yard people to do it, since they will be on the spot to do so.

Then at last you are back on your mooring, with your yacht freshly painted and varnished, all her gear checked and repaired or renewed where necessary, her engine over-hauled, her charts corrected, and so on. She is 'ready in all respects for sea'. Or you think she is. A short shakedown trip will probably reveal anything you've forgotten, or which isn't functioning properly.

Summer maintenance

There remains the question of maintenance during the sailing season. Provided that your fitting out was done properly, this should be minimal.

There is just one big job which may have to be done, and this is the mid-season cleaning off of her bottom. The rate of growth of weed, etc., on a yacht underwater varies from year to year (as well as from place to place) but at some stage during the summer the growth may have become such that something must be done about it. Weed in any quantity drastically cuts down a yacht's speed and responsiveness, and you won't be happy until you've got rid of it.

You can deal with the problem in one of two ways. You can get the yard to haul her out, scrub her off and give her a new coat of anti-fouling. This is by far the best way, of course, especially as it is a job they can do during the week. But it costs money.

Alternatively you can do it yourself. You can do this either by beaching your yacht at high water, if there is a suitable beaching ground available—a steep-to, clean shingle bank is best. Or you can find a berth for her up against a harbour wall, staging, piles etc., in a position where she will dry out. You can then get to work, but you will only be able to tackle one side at a time, and if she is of any size you will have to work pretty hard to get her new underwater coat on her between one tide and the next. You can do it in bits, of course, but it will still be a laborious business, and you are bound to lose a good deal of sailing time. All in all, you would be better advised to grit your teeth and put it on the yacht-yard bill.

There is no reason why your yacht should be out of the water during the season except to have her bottom cleaned, and even this may quite possibly not be necessary. Nor, except in the unfortunate event of her being damaged, should she have to undergo any repair which will immobilise her for any length of time. This is just as well. The summer is for sailing, and the number of good sailing days we get in an average season is far too small for anyone to want to miss even one of them. At the same time it must be emphasised that you should never postpone an important repair just because the sun is shining and a fair breeze blowing and you want to get out there and enjoy yourself. Always remember that, once you *are* out there, you must be prepared for anything.

Nor should you be slack about those humbler jobs which come under the heading of chores. It is only too easy to put these off, especially if you are tired after a passage, or if the weather is warm and tempts you to swim instead of swabbing down the decks. A yacht will very quickly become dirty and untidy both above and below decks if a regular cleaning and stowing routine is not maintained. On deck, slovenliness can become an actual hazard—for example, you might get into trouble if you found you couldn't slack off a sheet or a halliard in a hurry because it had got into a tangle or had been improperly secured; while below decks, where a number of people will probably be huddled together in conditions which ashore would amount to gross overcrowding, you can very quickly find yourself living in a slum. Some people don't seem to mind this—and a few even prefer it. The latter think it is 'tough' to ignore such things as neatness and cleanliness, as regards both the yacht and their own persons. They don't shave, or wash very often, and the yacht's accommodation is a grubby shambles. This may be in reaction to the clean and orderly life they have to lead ashore, but the fact of the matter is that what makes life pleasant on land goes for living aboard too, only more so. A clean and well-ordered ship is more likely than the other kind to be an efficient and happy ship.

While we are on the subject of putting things off, we may as well just mention the matter of keeping dry. It is easy to postpone the boring business of getting out your oilskins and putting them on when it starts to rain because 'it won't be much—it's only a shower'. On board a small yacht it is much easier to stay dry than to get dry again, and living in a state of more or less permanent dampness can be very depressing.

Remember too that you may need your oilskins even on a fine day—if, for example, you are beating in lively conditions and spray is coming inboard. It may be fun for a time, but you'll still end up wet. And you'll find it harder to get dry than if you'd been rained on, because of the salt content of the spray.

So—keep yourself clean and dry, and your ship clean and properly stowed. For the rest, let us very briefly sum up what the earlier pages of this book have tried to stress. Make sure everyone has proper meals and a good bunk (and enough time in it). Take care that your yacht is well-found in every respect. Get to know the waters you normally sail in as well as possible, and make a 'paper reconnaissance' of any new venture before you actually set out on it. Know the Rule of the Road, or as much of it as applies to you, and obey it when necessary (and don't leave anyone at the helm who doesn't know it, or only when it is absolutely safe to do so). Become as 'weather-wise' as you can, paying particular attention to local manifestations and effects. Decide what you, as skipper, require of your crew, and make sure that they know this too. Remember that the safety of all the 'souls' on board is in your care. Don't try to do anything you aren't sure you can manage, or that is beyond the capacity of the others on board.

With the exercise of a little care and common sense, your first season's cruising should be an enjoyable one. When it ends, and the yachting year ends too with the business of laying up, you will probably already be looking forward to next spring and getting afloat again. I hope so anyway!

11

Bon Voyage!

To CONCLUDE, we may perhaps just take a further look at a quality which at first sight may not seem to be essential to the make-up of the rugged seafarer. This is: consideration for others. This is in fact such an important aspect of yachting that a few cautionary words on the subject should not be out of place.

Many yachtsmen fail to show sufficient consideration towards their fellow mariners. This is a fault which naturally manifests itself in harbour rather than at sea, since it is only in harbour that you are likely to find yourself in close proximity to other vessels, whether they are other yachts or commercial craft.

You should take the greatest care never to manœuvre in harbour to the hazard of any of the vessels lying there. The yachtsman who regards an anchorage as a sort of obstacle course and charges about in it, perhaps under full sail, missing other craft by inches, is not likely to be popular. His skill in handling his vessel, however great it may be, will not be admired, and with good reason. The plain fact here is that it is not seamanlike to take chances.

Don't pick up someone else's mooring, then go off ashore and stay there for hours. The rightful occupant may be coming back soon. He may even be following you in. (That rude fellow isn't shouting at me, is he?)

If you want to secure outside another yacht or vessel which is lying alongside (a harbour wall, jetty, or staging) and which has no one aboard her, put someone ashore—or, if you are single-handed, go ashore yourself as soon as you can —to find out whether it is all right for you to lie there or not, and for how long. The other chap won't be too pleased if he wants to leave an hour later, and he has to shift your ship because you're in the pub, and he doesn't know who you are anyway.

When visiting another harbour or anchorage, try to find out, in advance if possible, whether there are any visitors'

moorings there. If you pick up one of these, find out as soon
as possible to whom you should pay the necessary dues, if
any. And pay them.

If it appears that you must anchor instead of picking up
a buoy, find out if this is in order, and where you can lie.
This is in your own interests as much as anyone else's, since
if you drop your hook on, say, a heap of old mooring chain
or some such clutter, you may not be able to get it again.
This will be most inconvenient, quite possibly expensive, and
will make you look pretty silly too.

If the harbour has a harbour-master, *do what he tells you.*
If he directs you to a certain berth or part of the harbour,
go there, and either anchor, pick up a buoy, or go alongside
as requested. If no harbour official is in evidence—and they
frequently aren't—find one as soon as you can, by going
to the harbour-master's office if necessary, and ask him where
you can lie. This, again, is a matter of common sense. If a
local fishing boat or tug or some other commercial craft
comes in in the middle of the night and finds you in her
berth, no one is going to be very happy. If no one comes to
collect your harbour dues, it is up to you to find out whether
there are any to pay, and whom to pay them to.

Take care to be on your very best behaviour in commercial
harbours. Yachtsmen are not beloved by those whose business
and livelihood is the sea, and we don't want to make ourselves more unpopular than we are already. Generally
speaking, the bigger and busier the harbour, the less welcome
the yachtsman will be; and the greater need for us to behave
ourselves.

To come nearer home, you should always show consideration not only to other craft and those who sail in them, but
to your own ship's company too. Remember that yachting is
something to be enjoyed, not only by you but by everyone
else on board too. This may perhaps seem too obvious to be
worth saying, but it is really most important. All too many
yacht owners, however mild and easy-going they may be
ashore, become evil-tempered tyrants the moment they get

afloat, bullying and frightening or antagonising everyone else on board.

In most cases, this kind of behaviour stems from the owner-skipper's own lack of confidence and knowledge of what he is about. All sorts of simple situations become emergencies and he shouts at everyone in an attempt to bluster his way through. The only-too-frequent result of this is to cause the others on board to panic too, which doesn't help at all.

Another common failing of newcomers to cruising is to try to do too much—for instance, to bash on for hours in bad weather when growing exhaustion and discomfort should have dictated that they seek shelter and a period of rest. Many do this in an effort to prove how rugged they are. This is not so bad if you are sailing with a bunch of like-minded people, but for most yachtsmen cruising is, or sooner or later becomes, a family affair, and not many wives and children take kindly to this sort of thing.

It will help if we accept the fact that, allowing for a few —a very few—exceptions, wives are not as mad keen to go rushing about the ocean as we are; and they will be even less keen if they find they are expected to do all the cooking and other domestic chores as well. So—don't frighten your 'mate' to death, or bring her to the verge of collapse. And *do* help with the preparing of meals, and the washing up, even if she does the actual cooking. (She may want to do this in self-defence anyway.) Otherwise you may find yourself sailing single-handed, which means you will be doing the lot.

Much the same applies in the case of children, though the chances are that they will be bored more often than they are frightened. Very young children don't present much of a problem, because you've only to park them somewhere safe and, unless they are sick, they will be as happy as they would be at home. But once they become at all mobile, the situation is very different. Until they are of an age to look after them-selves properly, they will either have to be confined below, or tethered safely above decks. Either way they are likely to fret at their enforced inactivity. They won't have anything to do, and there probably won't be much to see. Time passes very slowly for the young when they are not absorbed in anything, and a day's sail can seem endless to them.

A good deal of tolerance and restraint is called for here, but you will be repaid over and over again if you go about things the right way. There is nothing more gratifying than to find that your kids are developing the same enthusiasm for sailing that you have yourself. And such enthusiasm is not all that hard to foster. For example, all young children love a beach or an island. If you can find one or the other —preferably the one *on* the other—which you can sail to from your base in a reasonably short time, your worries will be half over. Going there will be an adventure, and they will appreciate the yacht because it gets them there. Your wife will probably enjoy it too. You may be a bit frustrated yourself, but if it gets too bad you can always have a rugged week-end with your male friends. The chances are that you won't enjoy that nearly as much.

Then, when your youngsters are a bit older, they can have fun with the dinghy. They can learn to row, and even to use the outboard. If you happen to have a sailing dinghy as a tender to your yacht, they can learn to sail that. That will be the best way of all of leading them in the way you want them to go.

Soon they will probably be telling you how to sail the yacht and by that time the battle will be won. Some time in their teens they will probably desert you to become dinghy-sailing fanatics, but that phase will pass. Before many years are out they will be thinking of cruising again, perhaps in a yacht of their own.

Which is more or less where we came in.

Bon voyage!

Index